The
The Jean an
Vanc

So NeaDated Yet So Far

By _____

So Near and Yet So Far

Rome, Canterbury and ARCIC

HUGH MONTEFIORE

SCM PRESS LTD

Cataloguing in Publication Data available

334 01517 0

First published 1986
by SCM Press Ltd
26–30 Tottenham Road London N1 4BZ

Typeset at The Spartan Press Ltd,
Lymington, Hants
and printed in Great Britain by
Billing & Sons Ltd,
Worcester

Contents

Foreword

This book is born from a strong desire for closer ecclesiastical relations between Anglicans and Roman Catholics, and from a conviction that the ARCIC Agreed Statements have left more unfinished business than what they have so magnificently achieved. An earlier slight essay that I wrote about ARCIC, published in *Theology*, drew from Professor Henry Chadwick the response that it had been composed in 'the excitement of rapidly composed polemic'. Certainly this book had to be rapidly composed against the remorseless headwind of an episcopal diary, if it was to see the light of day at all. It has also been exciting, as all theology is exciting. I am a convinced Anglican, and my most determined attempts at empathy with Roman Catholics are unlikely to be fully successful, but at least I have no conscious desire for polemics, only that by rigorous thinking as well as by prayer and life we shall together find that form of unity that God wants for his church.

Instead of quoting individual theologians, it seems more appropriate in this study to cite, so far as possible, only official statements or formularies of both churches.

St Matthias Day 1986   HUGH MONTEFIORE

1

The Miracle of Convergence

Viewed from the centre of the railway track, the two rails of the permanent way meet at a point, but the same track, seen from above, illustrates the adage that parallel lines never meet. The rules of perspective differ from the realities of life. This book is written to review the present relationship between Rome and Canterbury. There are those who look on that relationship from above, as it were, convinced that Rome and Canterbury run on parallel lines and that they will never converge as long as the sun and moon endure. The most that they would concede is that the broad-gauged track may become more narrow. On the other hand, there are those who, as it were, stand in the centre of the track, in danger of being run down by passing traffic but assured in their conviction that they can actually see ahead the point at which the rails converge. Extolling the virtues of the monorail system, in their mind's eye they can already see it operating. In writing this book, I take neither of these two stances, preferring a more detailed look at the rolling stock as it passes down the line, examining its features point by point, and especially the differences between different kinds of trains, bearing in mind the object of the journey as inscribed on the tombstone in memory of one William Pickering and Richard Edger outside Ely Cathedral:

> The line to heaven by Christ was made,
> With heavenly truth the Rails are laid,
> From Earth to Heaven the Line extends,
> To life eternal where it ends.

There can be no doubt of the great similarities between the Roman Catholic Church and the Church of England. Their members worship the same God, the Father, the Son and the Holy Spirit. They use the same creeds. They share in the one baptism. They are disciples of the same Christ, and they have all been made to share in the same Holy Spirit. What they have in common is far, far greater than what divides them.

Nonetheless, ever since the Reformation of the Church of England, until the very recent past, these two churches have looked upon each other as enemies. They have even killed each other's members in the name of God; Roman Catholic martyrs in the reign of Elizabeth and Protestant martyrs in the reign of Mary. During that short reign of Mary, any worship other than Roman Catholic was proscribed; but for a far longer period, after the Reformation of the Church of England, Roman Catholics were unable publicly to practice their faith, and later were expressly excluded from the Toleration Act of 1689. Catholic Emancipation, begun with an Act of very modest relief in 1778 (which nevertheless gave rise to the Gordon Riots), was not completed until this century, when an Act of 1926 removed any remaining disabilities, except those of holding certain offices in the state, or acting as patron of a Church of England benefice.

The history of the relationship between Canterbury and Rome over four centuries from the breach with Rome in 1559 through the Act of Supremacy down to the aftermath of the Second Vatican Council has been well told by Bernard and Margaret Pawley[1] and there is no need here to do more than draw attention to a few aspects which are important for this study. After the Reformation, the first rapprochement took place through correspondence between Archbishop Wake and French Roman Catholics (1717–20).[2] It proved abortive for two reasons; in the first place Wake, although Archbishop of Canterbury, was acting in a private capacity and he was corresponding with a group of dissident Roman Catholics rather than with authorized representatives – a very different state of affairs from today, when members of the Anglican-Roman Catholic International Commission are officially appointed by their churches. Secondly, Wake's correspondence tended to minimize important doctrinal differences – a matter to which the remaining chapters of this book are expressly directed.

In the next century conversations between Lord Halifax and

Abbé Portal which began in 1894 also failed, partly because these also were entirely unofficial, but overwhelmingly because the times were not ripe. Roman Catholicism then was triumphalist and expansionist; and the conversations abruptly drew to a close with the publication in 1896 of *Apostolicae Curae*, with its verdict that Anglican Orders were 'absolutely null and utterly void'. Talks began again in 1922 between Lord Halifax and Cardinal Mercier, after the Archbishops' Appeal to All Christian People in 1920 for unity had warmed the latter's heart.[3] These were still private talks, although this time they took place with the knowledge and encouragement of both the Pope and the Archbishop of Canterbury. But the talks ended with the death of Cardinal Mercier in 1926 and they were not resumed, because of pressures on both churches against reunion; on the Roman Catholic side, because the English Roman Catholic hierarchy objected, and on the side of the Church of England, because of the pressures (not unknown in the more recent past) of liturgical revision. Once again, the times were not ripe. The possibility of reunion between Rome and Canterbury had not yet gripped popular ecclesiastical imagination. The essential ecumenical preliminaries to enable such talks to be successful had not yet taken place; friendship and social intercourse between Anglicans and Roman Catholics, and co-operation rather than rivalry and mutual competition between the churches.

Twenty-five years ago, before the Roman Catholic Church had been instructed by the Second Vatican Council to be ecumenical, the atmosphere was still cold. The only prayer which Roman Catholics were permitted to say aloud with members of the Church of England was the Lord's Prayer. I remember, when I was Vicar of Great St Mary's, Cambridge, in the 1960s, engaging in a Jesuitical plot with Fr Tom Corbishley, SJ, to enable him to preach in that church. Sermons by Roman Catholics in Church of England parishes were not allowed by their hierarchy, so Fr Corbishley casually asked the Bishop of Northampton (who was away at the Vatican Council) if he could give an address in Great St Mary's – 'not part of liturgical worship'. The request was equally casually granted. I duly ended the brief undergraduate service with the blessing: we listened to a short piece by a string quartet, and then Fr Corbishley addressed the congregation. It was a moving occasion, perhaps the first of its kind, and Fr Corbishley began with an apology on behalf of his church: perhaps ecumenism would be the stronger if we could all do likewise.

The Vatican *Decree on Ecumenism* produced a sea change, containing a similar kind of confession:

> Christ summons the Church, as she goes her pilgrim way, to that continual reformation of which she always had need, insofar as she is an institution of men here on earth. Therefore, if the influence of events or of the times has led to deficiences in conduct, in Church discipline, or even in the formulation of doctrine, (which must be carefully distinguished from the deposit of faith itself) these should be appropriately rectified at the proper time.[4]

The Decree continues:

> There can be no ecumenism worthy of the name without a change of heart. For it is from newness of attitudes, from self-denial and unstinted love, that yearnings for unity may take their rise and grow towards maturity. We should therefore pray to the divine Spirit for the grace to be genuinely self-denying, humble, gentle in the service of others and to have an attitude of brotherly generosity towards them.[5]

The Decree ends with a plea for genuine ecumenism:

> This most sacred synod urgently desires that the initiatives of the sons of the Catholic Church, joined with those of the separated brethren, go forward without obstructing the ways of divine Providence and without prejudging the future intention of the Holy Spirit.[6]

This urgent summons produced its effect, although inevitably some of the older church leaders found it hard to change their ways overnight. Cardinal Heenan, addressing the Church Leaders Conference held in Birmingham in September 1972, disappointed his hearers, reporting that the great majority of English Roman Catholics, while they wished to be friendly with non-Catholics, did not wish to worship in their churches; and 'they have no interest in what we call ecumenical dialogue'.[7] Bishop B. C. Butler, former Abbot of Downside, preaching in Great St Mary's in the late 1960s (no stratagems were needed for this preaching engagement) said: 'Now that the Roman Catholic Church has moved in on the ecumenical movement in rather a big way, there is a certain amount of hesitation and anxiety among the "old campaigners".'[8]

The appointment of Basil Hume as Heenan's successor heralded a new era for Roman Catholicism in England. In the first place, the Cardinal was clearly an Englishman, whereas the dominant image of the Roman Catholic in England had previously been Irish. The Cardinal's ascetic face, so photogenic on television, together with his gentle voice and deep spirituality, endeared him to the English people as a whole: and (aided perhaps by *The Times* ecclesiastical correspondent, himself a Roman Catholic) that church took on a higher profile in the national life of England. Cardinal Hume, for example, became President of Shelter, the housing pressure group. Relationships between the two churches grew warmer and friendlier. In 1888 G. D. Salmon had written *The Infallibility of the Church* in which he spoke of those who became Roman Catholics as having not a conversion but a perversion to Rome. As late as 1952 this book was reissued:[9] but by the 1980s such language was unthinkable. Similarly in 1948 Richard Hanson and Reginald Fuller wrote *The Church of Rome: A Dissuasive*. In its introduction they asked: 'Why write a Dissuasive at all? Why not an Eirenicon?', and they went on to remark: 'We are convinced that numbers of people go over because they are dazzled in one way or another by the "Grandeur that is Rome".'[10] I do not think that they would write in this way today. In the same way I do not think that Roman Catholics today would describe members of the Church of England as 'a sect in manifest heresy and delusion and as such as hateful as the contradictions of Korah, Dathan and Abiram', as *The Tablet* wrote in 1897.[11]

There are many reasons for the growing together of the two churches in this land. In the first place, the Roman Catholic Church itself seems to have become more Anglican. Many of the difficulties which forced our distant ancestors to take the extreme step of severance with Rome seem to have been recognized by Rome and put right. The use of the 'vulgar tongue' in liturgy, the encouragement of parish councils, the restoration of the chalice to the laity (more evident perhaps on the continent of Europe than in England), the use of public services of reconciliation in place of private confession, the growing obsolescence of the service of Benediction (now more common in Anglo-Catholic than in English Roman Catholic circles), the supersession of private masses by concelebration, the use of the sacrament of Unction generally for healing rather than exclusively as part of the Last Rites, the

encouragement of biblical scholarship including the use of higher
criticism of the Bible, the disuse (for the most part) of theological
censorship and the reform (at least in name) of the Holy Office, the
desuetude of Indulgences and the growth of a Christ-centred
Mariology – all these have resulted in the Roman Catholic Church
appearing to come closer both to Anglican ethos and to Anglican
practice. In particular, the similarity between the eucharistic rites of
the two churches must be stressed. The ordinary lay person,
unversed in the liturgical niceties and intricacies of eucharistic
theology, might well think that the two rites are interchangeable.

From another perspective matters look very different. The
similarities between their two eucharistic rites could be put down to
Roman influence on Anglican liturgists rather than *vice versa*. Since
the Oxford Movement a century ago the Church of England has
been deepening its sacramental life. The growth of the parish
communion movement has resulted in its becoming the main
(perhaps the only) Sunday service in the Church of England. There
has been a renewal in religious life, so that since Vatican II Anglican
and Roman Catholic religious orders have grown closer together.
Within Anglican circles there has been a growth of interest in
catholic spirituality, not least in the practice of meditation and
contemplation. There has been a concern within the Church of
England too with ecclesiology, beginning with the Reports *Catholicity* and *The Fullness of Christ* (commissioned by Archbishop
Geoffrey Fisher after the Second Great War), and with the
publication in 1950 of *Church Relations in England*; and this has
been deepened by negotiations with the Methodist Church, and
over the Ten Propositions, as well as by ARCIC. The Church of
England has become more conscious of itself as a church, not least
in its relations with the state, particularly over the appointment of
bishops. Synodical government has meant the formal recognition of
the episcopal college; and the strengthening of the Anglican
Communion through the Anglican Consultative Council and
Primates' Meetings has meant a fuller recognition of the universal
church. If the Roman church has become more Anglican, the
Anglican Communion has grown more catholic. Furthermore
the new Anglican rite is very similar to the Roman Mass. In
addition to these liturgical convergences, there are pastoral convergences too. In 1980 there was held the National Pastoral Congress
involving twenty Roman Catholic dioceses of England and Wales,

as well as the religious orders and other groups. Although the official publication of the Conference was *The Easter People*,[12] a message from the Roman Catholic bishops of England and Wales, rather than from the Congress itself, and although some of the Congress recommendations seem to have fallen by the wayside, nonetheless for the first time the lay members of the Roman Catholic Church were involved if not in decision-taking, at least in the process of decision-making, just as they are in Roman Catholic Pastoral Councils; a process not wholly dissimilar from the work of Parochial Church Councils, Deanery Synods, Diocesan Synods and the General Synod of the Church of England. The involvement of the laity in the work of the church is perhaps not so evident in the Roman Catholic Church of this country, where English priests may be augmented by those lent by Irish dioceses; but in other countries, where the shortage of priests is acute, the pastoral work of the laity is more evident. In the diocese of Lyon for example (the city of Lyon is twinned with Birmingham), the shortage is so acute that lay people prepare parents for baptism, children for confirmation and couples for marriage.

Furthermore, there is now pastoral consultation between hierarchies. Following on from the recommendation of the Malta Conference in 1968,[13] joint meetings of local hierarchies take place annually, where friendships are formed and pastoral problems are aired; and (at least in the West Midlands) these meetings are helpful and fruitful. Furthermore, the Roman Catholic bishops of England and Wales permit the making of local covenants as an ecumenical way forward where Roman Catholic parishes and other congregations agree to co-operate and to work together as much as is permissible, and in some cases to share the same building for worship; and in the light of this, Roman Catholics often form part of regional sponsoring bodies for local ecumenical projects.

Even more striking, perhaps, is the personal co-operation between church leaders. The Archbishop of Canterbury, it is known, regularly consults with Cardinal Hume before making a public utterance; and the remarkable partnership in Liverpool between David Sheppard and Derek Warlock, Anglican Bishop and Roman Catholic Archbishop, is so well-known that the average Liverpudlian, asked what is meant by ecumenism, would probably reply, 'Them two bishops'.

The two bishops in Liverpool have co-operated closely on the difficult social problems associated with that city. In addition to such local co-operation there is contact between the Board for Social Responsibility of the Church of England and the relevant committees of the Episcopal Conference of England and Wales on matters of social responsibility. An example of such co-operation is the united stand by both churches against the total deregulation of Sunday trading; and further steps in co-operation are in process of being planned. Although there are some serious differences on matters of personal and social ethics, nonetheless there are areas where the two churches can co-operate closely. In addition, mutual help is afforded by the prophetic witness of individuals. Mother Teresa, for example, in her loving care for the dying in Calcutta, has aroused the consciences of multitudes, both Roman Catholic and non-Catholic; and in South Africa the witness of Archbishop Hurley in the Roman Catholic Church as well as Archbishop Desmond Tutu in the Anglican Church of the province of South Africa have afforded encouragement to Christians of other churches than their own. This all tends to draw Anglicans and Roman Catholics closer together.

There is a further important factor which must be mentioned. The charismatic movement seems to have made its first significant impact on Anglicanism in the parish of St Mark Van Nuys in California, under the ministry of Dennis Bennett in 1958–60.[14] By 1962 the phenomena connected with the movement were evident within the Church of England, and it has influenced many parishes. One of the distinctive characteristics of the movement is love and openness not only towards individuals but also towards members of other churches. The same movement has greatly influenced parishes of the Roman Catholic Church in England as elsewhere. This has led to a mutual openness and understanding between members of both churches, which has helped to foster mutual understanding and sometimes a 'divine discontent' with the separation between the two ecclesiastical bodies viewed as human institutions. Furthermore, in addition to the charismatic movement itself, there has been within the Church of England not only a new Evangelical awakening, but also a new openness within the Evangelical wing of the Church of England to what is good in other traditions. These factors all contribute to the evident drawing together of Christians from both churches. Furthermore, it is evident that the world becomes more and more secular; and in a situation in which England has become a missionary country, the minority who are committed Christians feel a divine impulse to come together and to make a joint witness to an increasingly godless world.

Nor should the importance of national occasions be forgotten. When a national service is arranged, it is normal nowadays for the Cardinal to be involved as well as the Archbishop of Canterbury; and it may not be so well known that, although the Archbishop of Canterbury is thought to be responsible for the sober and non-triumphalist tone of the Falkland Island Service at St Paul's Cathedral, in fact the Cardinal Archbishop (together with the Moderator of the Free Church Federal Council) were only prepared to participate on such conditions, a factor which greatly strengthened the Archbishop's hand.

All these factors have tended to bring together the two churches in this land. But the Roman Catholic Church is far bigger than England (just as, on a smaller scale, the Anglican Communion is far larger than the Church of England, even if the Anglican Communion sometimes wonders whether the Church of England is aware of this fact). The Pope sends to each country his own personal representative, and the upgrading of Bruno Heim from being Apostolic Delegate to Papal Pro Nuncio (a move which afforded him full diplomatic status) appeared to set the seal of government approval on a new relationship. The personalities of recent Popes have helped towards this relationship. Pope John XXIII was a saintly man, charged by God with calling an ecumenical council of an altogether new kind, which produced constitutions rather than infallible decrees, and to which members of other churches were invited as observers. I remember attending a general audience of John XXIII at a time when he was mortally ill. He began in a frail and tremulous manner, and an aide was by his side to assist him if he stumbled or felt faint. But as the Pope warmed to his apostolic discourse, so the Spirit renewed his strength, and he ended with power and with humour, evoking laughter and applause through his references to his beloved San Giuseppe.

Paul VI was also a remarkable Pope, less extrovert than John XXIII (although the latter's *Journal of a Soul*[15] shows him to have been a person of interior depth). Paul VI agonized over the world's problems, and over the divisions within the church; but he was also a person of rare understanding and great humility. I remember, on an occasion when I and my wife were granted a private audience with him, how, although he had just had an exhausting round of both public and private audiences, he was keen to discuss student religion; and when I knelt down at the beginning of the audience to ask for his blessing, he said: 'Get up! I am a human being like yourself!'

It is, however, the present Pope John Paul II who has most captured popular imagination. His many visits overseas, the attempt at his assassination which so nearly proved fatal, and his forgiveness of his would-be assassin, together with his care for the disabled, his love of young people, and his insistence on human rights, have all endeared him to multitudes. Himself once an actor, his ability to handle huge crowds assists his public image. A major factor in the drawing closer of the Church of England and the Roman Catholic Church was his visit to this country in 1982 and his visit to Canterbury Cathedral on that occasion.

However, it must be realized that in a sense he was repaying visits by earlier Archbishops of Canterbury to his predecessors. In 1960, at the age of 73, Archbishop Geoffrey Fisher announced visits to Jerusalem, Istanbul and Rome.[16] This was to be the first encounter between a Pope and an Archbishop of Canterbury since Archbishop Arundel visited the Vatican in 1397.[17] Fisher pulled up Pope John XXIII when he read from an address he had given about 'the time when our separated brethren should return to the Mother Church', and from that time onwards there was no more talk about returning to a past situation.[18] In 1966 Archbishop Michael Ramsey visited the Vatican and together with the Pope they signed a Common Declaration. Later in 1977 Archbishop Donald Coggan also went to visit the Pope in the Vatican, and was greeted with the same warmth and a further Common Declaration was made.

And so, when Pope John Paul II came to visit Canterbury Cathedral, it was in a sense a return visit for those occasions of prayer in the Sistine Chapel. But this was different. Despite difficulties over precedence between Archbishop Marcinkus and the Canterbury Chapter the previous night, the Pope and the Archbishop were obviously seen to be equals, with the host giving precedence to the guest, and the guest in turn deferring to his host. The Pope took part in a public service which was not under his control or jurisdiction. He publicly recognized Dr Runcie as Archbishop of Canterbury, implying that he was not a mere layman

whose priestly orders were 'absolutely void and utterly null'. I
myself shall long treasure the fatherly embrace that he gave me on
both cheeks, as he greeted the whole college of diocesan bishops
of the Church of England, and the way in which he addressed the
whole congregation as his brothers and sisters in Christ with whom
he shared a common baptism. The Pope himself seemed impressed
by the unique nature of the occasion as well as by the Gothic
beauties and ordered catholic worship of Canterbury Cathedral.

In view of the attractiveness of these church leaders, and the
rapport which they established by their meetings in Rome or in
Canterbury, it is necessary to examine with special care the
theological basis for a rapprochement.

There has been a repeated request for reciprocal communion to
be permitted on occasion between the two churches. Cardinal
Heenan, asked at the Birmingham Church Leaders Conference in
1972 whether in the not too distant future non-Catholics might be
allowed to receive communion in his church, replied that he could
only conceive of that in the most unfavourable circumstances,
maybe in a concentration camp; whereupon Canon Bernard
Pawley a great admirer of the Roman Catholic Church, who was
chairing the meeting, responded: 'It seems then that we should
pray for a multiplication of concentration camps'.[19] Officially the
situation has not greatly changed. Archbishop Donald Coggan
made the plea more official when he reiterated it on his official
visit to the Vatican in 1977; and it met with polite but firm
disapproval. It is well known, however, that communion is often
privately offered to non-Catholics at Catholic retreats and in
religious houses, certainly on the continent; but I heard only
recently of a Roman Catholic priest, inwardly moved to receive
communion at an Anglican altar, being told by his diocesan who
learnt about it that he would never receive preferment (a judgment which no doubt considerably relieved him). Until Roman
Catholics officially believe that a eucharist celebrated by an Anglican priest is a real eucharist, and that the priest's orders are valid,
it is unrealistic to expect them to encourage such participation;
and, so far as their own eucharists are concerned, they believe that
participation in eucharistic fellowship should be the result of union
rather than a means towards it; and (except for pressing pastoral
reasons) they are unwilling to anticipate the conclusion of our
efforts towards unity.

Among all this evidence of convergence, there is one initiative which seems to lead in a different direction. In 1970 Pope Paul VI canonized forty English martyrs of the Reformation era. A further eighty-five are in process of being canonized and are expected shortly to reach the status of 'blessed'. Although Roman Catholics, after the Pope had released them from loyalty to their Queen, were subject to the political charge of high treason, there were undoubtedly among these martyrs godly, good and brave men. The same, however, could be said of those Protestants who were martyred in the reign of Queen Mary, of whom only Cranmer, Latimer and Ridley feature in the calendar of the Church of England. (There were 288 Marian martyrs during the four years of her reign, and 188 Roman Catholics martyred in Elizabeth's reign between 1577 and 1603.)[20] Perhaps once the Roman Catholic mechanism for beatification gets into gear, it cannot be reversed. It is hard to see how these moves will assist ecumenism, and it must be hoped that English Roman Catholics will feel sufficiently secure not to need to draw strength from their unhappy past.

So far as mixed marriages are concerned, the Roman Catholic discipline rests upon rather different premises in addition to the same doctrine of the church as is involved in the refusal of intercommunion. The *motu proprio Matrimonia Mixta* of 1970 gave some relaxation of earlier discipline, but it still required the Roman Catholic partner 'to do all that can be done' to provide *pro viribus* for the Roman Catholic education of the children of the marriage, although it dispensed with the requirement of a signed statement to this effect.[21] This rests upon a doctrine of the church which a member of the Church of England cannot be expected to accept, as though baptism in the Church of England is less Christian than in the Roman Catholic Church. (The promises could also be said to be insensitive to the conscience of the committed Anglican partner, and to involve decisions which ought properly to be taken not unilaterally but by the partners together.) The *motu proprio* does not permit that the marriage be solemnized in the Church of England rather than in the Roman Catholic Church as a general law, but only by special dispensation; nor is there provision for the couple to share communion on such a special occasion. These Roman Catholic regulations do still cause some offence to committed members of the Church of England who are affected by them, but at the same time the relaxation of earlier regulations has meant that the offence is not so great as it used to be.

The Common Declaration made by Pope Paul VI and Archbishop Michael Ramsey in 1966 did not envisage the possibility of intercommunion as a means towards reunion, but rather a dialogue which should cover scripture, tradition, liturgy and matters of practical difficulty, aware that 'serious obstacles stand in the way of a restoration of complete communion of faith and sacramental life'.

> In willing obedience to the command of Christ Who bade His disciples love one another, they declare that, with His help, they wish to leave in the hands of the God of mercy all that in the past has been opposed to this precept of charity, and that they make their own the mind of the Apostle which he expressed in these words: 'Forgetting those things which are behind, and reaching forth unto those things which are before, I press towards the mark for the prize of the high calling of God in Christ Jesus' (cf. Phil. 3.13–14).[22]

As a result of this historic declaration, the Anglican/Roman Catholic Joint Preparatory Commission met twice in 1967 and in 1968 and issued what is known as the Malta Report. This Report recommended progress by stages. The first stage would be one of dialogue, with suggestions about subjects (which were not in fact followed up) and about two permanent sub-commissions (one concerned with intercommunion and the other with the nature of authority) which again were not followed up. However, the permanent commission recommended in the Report was set up, and ten of the further recommendations are being implemented, the only exception being the institution at international level of an official joint consultation to consider the difficulties involved and the co-operation which should be undertaken in the field of missionary strategy and activity.

As a result of the Malta Report, the Anglican-Roman Catholic International Commission was set up, which produced in turn the Windsor Statement on Eucharistic Doctrine (1971), the Canterbury Statement on Ministry and Ordination (1973), and the Venice Statement on Authority in the Church (1976), and the Salisbury Statement called Elucidations (1979) and a Final Report (1982). Since then the old ARCIC went out of existence, and a new Commission has been set up.

These Statements are being considered by the two Communions. The Church of England, in General Synod on 14 February 1985, made a preliminary response by recognizing that the first two Statements (together with the Elucidations) are consonant in substance with the faith of the Church of England and that the Venice Statement on Authority I, together with its Elucidation, and Authority II, record sufficient convergence on the nature of authority in the church for the two communions to explore further the structures of authority and the exercise of collegiality and primacy in the church. Responses by the various churches and provinces of the Anglican Communion are to be collated by the Anglican Consultative Council and to be submitted to the Lambeth Conference which is due to take place in 1988. Similarly the Roman Catholic Church has asked Episcopal Conferences to comment on the Agreed Statements, after Cardinal Ratzinger, on behalf of the Congregation of the Doctrine of the Faith, issued a somewhat critical welcome.

It is easy to forget that this dialogue between the Anglican Communion and the Roman Catholic Church is not the only series of discussions on which the Roman Catholic Church (or the Anglican Communion)[23] is engaged. The most important item on the Roman Catholic ecumenical agenda is reconciliation between itself and the Orthodox Churches. It is also engaged in discussion with the Methodist Churches, the Lutheran Churches and the Reformed Churches. It is all too easy for Anglicans to imagine that they have a special place in Roman Catholic ecumenism.

It is also easy for members of the Church of England to imagine that reunion with the Roman Catholic Church is 'just round the corner'.[24] A warmth of mutual fellowship and affection has been generated so quickly, and so much reconciliation has been already achieved in so short a time, that a foreshortening of what still lies ahead is easily effected. The convergence achieved from the ARCIC discussions has been truly miraculous, in the sense that it could never have been foreseen, and is something truly to be wondered at. So much has been achieved in so brief a period compared with past centuries of apartheid and mutual incomprehension, so that progress to date must be attributed not only to the efforts of individuals, but also to the inspiration and guidance of the Holy Spirit.

At the same time it must not be forgotten that within the last decade the Church of England has also grown very close to the Methodist Church, and despite high hopes, the scheme between the two churches failed, although there was a very large measure of agreement indeed on doctrinal matters. Since then a further move towards reunion based on the Ten Propositions has likewise come to nothing. These two failures have left many members of the Church of England not only with a feeling of failure, but also with a determination not to renege on their brothers and sisters in Christ in the Free Churches of this land, to whom the Church of England in the past has been closer than to the Roman Catholic Church. Such people are determined that an understanding with the Roman Catholic Church must not be at the expense of a similar understanding with the Free Churches.

Apart from this, grave and difficult theological problems still face Anglicans and Roman Catholics. In the euphoria caused by progress so far, it is vital that these difficulties should not be overlooked, or once again the Church of England will have to draw back from the brink of commitment. In the chapters that follow an attempt will be made to subject these theological difficulties to brief examination.

2

The Church and its
Sources of Authority

When Dr Eric Kemp, the Bishop of Chichester, was speaking in
General Synod in February 1985 with reference to the response that
the Church of England should make to the ARCIC Agreed
Statements, he described them as follows:

> They try to move away from the confessional formulations of the
> last 400 years and to see the questions at issue in the light of
> Scripture and of the understanding and practice of the Church
> before the great divisions of East and West. They must therefore
> be examined in terms of what they have tried to do rather than be
> brought to the bar of our own Anglican formularies. We must not
> act like the judicial committee of the Privy Council in the
> nineteenth-century doctrine cases and try to compare passages
> from the report with passages from the Articles and Prayer Book,
> to see whether there is a verbal consistency. We are asked to
> consider more broadly whether in one case we can 'recognize the
> faith of the Church through the ages' (with reference to Euchar-
> istic Doctrine, and Ministry and Ordination) and in another (with
> reference to Authority) whether what is said 'is consonant in
> substance with the faith of the Church of England'.[1]

The result of this approach is there is an obvious 'difference
between the ideal and the actual'.[2] Some years ago I ventured to
remark that a sentence in the Venice Statement was 'typical of the

Report, in so far as it confuses what *ought* to be the case with what *is* the case'.[3] Dr Henry Chadwick, responding to this remark, asked: 'Is this complaint really as damaging as it may seem to those who have never tried to construct a doctrine of the church in coherent terms? A satisfactory exposition of the essential being of the church can hardly be attempted at all if the data available exclude any element of the ideal and heavenly and are strictly confined to the not too militant community of frail believers whose treasure is in very earthen vessels.'[4]

Dr Chadwick defends the method of ARCIC in robust language which deserves a lengthy quotation:

It is self-evident that the Venice Statement sets forth what the church in general, and within the church primacy, ought to be. The point is underlined expressly in the co-chairmen's preface: 'An awareness of this distinction between the ideal and the actual is important both for the reading of the document and for the understanding of the method we have pursued.' And the antithesis between what ought to be and what is emerges several times in the course of the document itself. But at the back of the not very pertinent complaint about ought and is there lies perhaps a deeper difference. The greatest of all differences between Bishop Montefiore and ARCIC seems to lie in the dimension of the Holy Spirit's living presence and continued activity within the community of God's people in time and space. The virtual absence of this dimension from his discussion of these thorny problems, other than as a sanctification of tolerance amid dissension, gives a static look to his view of the ecumenical task, so as to make it almost an apotheosis of the deaf . . .[5]

Such a long quotation may perhaps be justified by a need to be fair to one's critic. I do not deny there is some substance in Dr Chadwick's remarks. If ecumenism means a meeting of minds and hearts, and a common openness to the truth wherever it leads, we must not expect that the goal of reunion will be either an absorption of one view by another, or a mere agreement to differ: the way must be open under the guidance of the Spirit, for movement on *both* sides of a divide, in so far as that is possible in accordance with the principles on which either side may operate. Put in non-theological categories, it is as well to set out the goal of a common journey (the

ideal) before deciding how best (or even perhaps how possible it is)
to move from one's actual position.

It follows that, as a method, the attempt to set forth an ideal (such
as the Agreed Statements attempt) at least for Anglicans may be a
helpful preliminary so long as it is realized that this is only an early
stage of the ecumenical process, and that there lies ahead the task
for both parties of moving from the actual (and the situations in
which actual churches find themselves are governed by formularies,
canon law, sentiment, custom and their understanding of truth)
onwards to the joint realization of a common ideal. Theologically
speaking this suggests two separable tasks; first, a theological
critique of the Agreed Statements, and secondly, a comparison of
the theology of these Agreed Statements with the particular
doctrines of the two communions. (There remains a further task of
considering doctrines concerning faith and morals not actually
mentioned in the Agreed Statements.)

Before considering Christian doctrine, it is necessary for its
proper evaluation to consider the sources of authority for the
formation of Christian doctrine. Unless there is agreement on these
sources of authority, there is unlikely to be agreement about the
resulting theology. Professor Lampe, when speaking about
Authority I in the General Synod, spoke some words which
his premature death sadly prevented him from developing. He
said of the Statement:

> It is not about authority in the church: it is almost entirely about
> who exercises it. The great prior theological questions are: what is
> the nature of authority, especially in matters of belief? What is its
> source? What do we mean by revelation? What is the relation of
> revelation to doctrine? These questions represent the great divi-
> sive issue of the present time, an issue which sometimes makes
> liberal Christianity and authoritarian Christianity look almost like
> two different religions. Until that issue is explored thoroughly,
> there is little point in talking about councils and primates.[6]

Professor Lampe spoke those words in 1977, and the previous
year the Doctrine Commission of the Church of England had issued
its Report, after much difficulty and disagreement, entitled *Christian Believing*.[7] As a fellow member of the Doctrine Commission my
own feelings were similar to his, and I said, in the same debate: 'It
would have been better for this Synod to have considered our own

Anglican ways of believing before addressing itself to this Anglican-
Roman Catholic Agreed Statement.'[8] However, the important
issues raised by the Report *Christian Believing* were ignored in the
Church of England until they erupted (amid thunderous publicity)
when Dr David Jenkins was raised to the episcopate and became
Bishop of Durham in 1984.

Professor Lampe's remarks, however, were scarcely fair to the
ARCIC statements on Authority when amplified by the later
Elucidations. In Authority I it is said of the New Testament:

> They preached Jesus through whom God has spoken finally to
> men. Assisted by the Holy Spirit they transmitted what they had
> heard and seen of the life and words of Jesus and their
> interpretation of his redemptive work. Consequently the inspired
> documents in which this is related came to be accepted by the
> Church as a normative record of the authentic foundation of the
> faith. To these the Church has recourse for the inspiration of its
> life and mission; to these the Church refers its teaching and
> practice. Through these written words the authority of the Word
> of God is conveyed. Entrusted with these documents, the
> Christian community is enabled by the Holy Spirit to live out the
> Gospel and so to be led into all truth.[9]

The chief source of authority in matters of belief is here clearly
spelled out. These statements place scripture, and in particular the
New Testament, in a position of pre-eminence as 'a normative
record of the authentic foundation of their faith' – a phrase which is
further expounded in the Elucidation.[10] A close connection is made
between scripture and tradition. According to the Agreed Statement Authority I the decisions of General Councils are authoritative and binding on the whole church when they express the
common faith and mind of the whole church; but the decisions of
such councils are only preserved from error about fundamental
matters of faith which formulate the central truths of our salvation,
and which are faithful to scripture and consistent with tradition.[11]

ARCIC clearly sees tradition as a further source of authority,
although subservient to scripture. However Cardinal Ratzinger,
Prefect of the Sacred Congregation for the Doctrine of Faith,
writing in his private capacity, regards this as the wrong way to
understand tradition. 'In the Catholic Church, the principle of
tradition refers, not only and not even in the first place, to the

permanency of ancient texts or documents which have been handed down, but to a certain way of co-ordinating the living word of the church and the decisive written word of scripture. Here "tradition" means above all, that the church, living in the form of the apostolic succession with the Petrine office at its centre, is the place in which the Bible is lived and interpreted in a way that binds.'[12] If Cardinal Ratzinger's view of tradition is decisive, then of course the whole logic of the Agreed Statements collapses.

The Elucidation (on which Professor Lampe did not live to comment) also refers to the relation of doctrine to revelation. God who has disclosed himself by speaking through the patriarchs and prophets, summed up his self-disclosure by speaking his final Word through Jesus Christ. It is clear from this that revelation is understood not primarily as abstract propositions divinely revealed but as God's self-disclosure spoken through chosen persons, and finally through his Son. The doctrinal task is 'to unfold the full extent and implications of the mystery of Christ, under the guidance of the Spirit of the risen Lord'.[13] For this, the formulation of creeds, conciliar definitions and other statements of belief have been found to be indispensable, but 'these are always instrumental to the truth which they are intended to convey'.[14] It is not possible, on such a view, to add to the content of revelation, but only to emphasize some important truth, to expound the faith more lucidly, to draw out implications not sufficiently recognized, and to show how Christian truth applies to contemporary issues.

According to Authority I authoritative statements can be made for these purposes not merely by synodical means, but also by a universal primate:

> The welfare of the *koinonia* does not require that all the statements of those who speak authoritatively on behalf of the Church should be considered permanent expressions of the truth. But situations may occur where serious divisions of opinion on crucial issues of pastoral urgency call for a more definitive judgment. Any such statement would be intended as an expression of the mind of the church . . . All such definitions are provoked by specific historical situations and are always made in terms of the understanding and framework of their age. But in the continuing life of the Church they retain a lasting significance . . .[15]

The Agreed Statements would seem to contain a coherent view of the sources of authority for Christian doctrine, majoring on the scriptures as containing the normative account of the authentic foundation of our faith and recording God's revelation which was spoken through the prophets and patriarchs and which culminated in his final Word in Jesus Christ. The findings of ecumenical councils, when they deal with fundamental matters of faith which formulate the central truths of our salvation, are preserved from error and are binding on the church in so far as they amplify and elucidate the doctrines of the New Testament; and at critical times of pastoral necessity a universal primate may express the mind of the church without recourse to an ecumenical council which would take time and preparation to bring into being.

Such a simple statement, however, hides a number of very difficult problems. On what grounds (other than usage) is scripture regarded as normative? Does it adequately convey in propositional form the revelation which God has spoken through people? Does God always reveal himself through words, or does he speak through personality and through events? On what grounds is scripture held to be the 'uniquely inspired witness to divine revelation'?[16] What are the criteria by which it may be decided whether a council has legitimately interpreted what may be *implied* by New Testament doctrines? (As Cardinal Ratzinger points out, if there were such a thing as 'manifestly legitimate', there would be no need of teaching authority.)[17] How can a universal primate be said to have expressed the mind of the church without recourse to an ecumenical council if his pronouncements (e.g. in *Humanae Vitae* on the subject of birth control) are not received by the people of God as expressing the mind of the church? If 'reception does not create truth nor legitimize the decision' but only provides 'the final indication that such a decision has fulfilled the necessary conditions for it to be a true expression' of faith or morals,[18] in what way have the necessary conditions not been met (e.g. in the case of *Humanae Vitae*)? Are beliefs (e.g. the uniqueness of scripture, or the preservation from error of the findings of ecumenical councils under certain conditions) to be understood as dogmas which have been divinely revealed to the church (but divine revelation is said to have ended with God's final Word to man in Jesus Christ), or are they open questions which may legitimately be questioned and criticized within the church? It is precisely these kinds of questions which show the divide between liberal Christianity and authoritarian Christianity of which Professor Lampe spoke.

Somewhat similar divisions are to be found in both the Roman Catholic and within the Anglican Communion; and they have not been finally resolved in either, although each church has a different way of approaching them, and a different discipline in dealing with those who raise such critical questions. Perhaps they can only be solved by the clearer guidance of the Holy Spirit of God.

So far as the Roman Catholic Church is concerned, the relationship between scripture and tradition is expounded in the Schema on *Divine Revelation*, God is a personal God who has spoken to men. He has initiated a dialogue with them in which they are invited to listen to his words and to respond. His words are revelation and man's response is faith. Revelation is a manifestation by God – granted to particular men at particular times. Every single such communication is part of a larger pattern. Revelation by its nature is public. Therefore it has to be made known to others by the testimony of its recipient. Passed on orally it becomes tradition; recorded in writing, it becomes scripture.[19] Two key sections in the *Constitution on Divine Revelation* deserve to be quoted in full. The first concerns scripture and tradition:

> There exist a close connection and communication between sacred tradition and sacred Scripture. For both of them, flowing from the same divine wellspring, in a certain way merge into a unity and tend toward the same end. For sacred Scripture is the word of God inasmuch as it is consigned to writing under the inspiration of the divine Spirit. To the successors of the apostles sacred tradition hands on in its full purity God's word, which was entrusted to the apostles by Christ the Lord and the Holy Spirit. Thus led by the light of the Spirit of truth, these successors can in their preaching preserve this word of God faithfully, explain it, and make it more widely known. Consequently it is not from sacred Scripture alone that the Church draws her certainty about everything that has been revealed. Therefore both sacred tradition and sacred Scripture are to be accepted and venerated with the same sense of devotion and reverence.[20]

Vatican II put scripture on the same level as tradition. Perhaps there is no formal contradiction between this statement and the passage cited earlier from the Agreed Statement on Authority I, in so far as the Vatican II Constitution does not deny that scripture is a normative record; but on the other hand the Agreed Statement appears to treat tradition (except in certain clearly defined conditions) as on a rather lower level than scripture.

In a second passage the relationship of scripture and tradition to the magisterium of the church is spelled out:

> Sacred tradition and sacred Scripture form one sacred deposit of the word of God, which is committed to the Church. Holding fast to this deposit, the entire holy people united with their shepherds remain always steadfast in the teaching of the apostles, in the common life, in the breaking of the bread and in prayers, so that in holding to, practising and professing the heritage of faith, there results on the part of the bishops and faithful a remarkable common effort.
>
> The task of authentically interpreting the word of God, whether written or handed on, has been entrusted exclusively to the living teaching office of the Church, whose authority is exercised in the name of Jesus Christ. This teaching office is not above the word of God but serves it, teaching only what has been handed on, listening to it devoutly, guarding it scrupulously and explaining it faithfully by divine commission and with the help of the Holy Spirit; it draws from this one deposit of faith everything which it presents for belief as divinely revealed.
>
> It is clear therefore that sacred tradition, sacred Scripture and the teaching authority of the Church, in accord with God's most wise design, are so linked and joined together that one cannot stand without the others, and that all together and each in its own way under the action of the one Holy Spirit contribute effectively to the salvation of souls.[21]

This lengthy quotation is needed to clarify the approach of the Roman Catholic Church which is very different from that of the Anglican Communion, at least in so far as the magisterium of the church is concerned. The teaching authority of the church is not specifically defined in this quotation, but the magisterium consists of the bishops and supremely of the Pope. No license is given here to the Christian scholar to pursue the truth wherever it may lead, just as in the sections dealing with biblical research nothing is said about the biblical theologians' liberty of research. Although the methods by which the Congregation of the Doctrine of the Faith work have greatly changed, their task of maintaining purity of doctrine still remains. Professor Hans Küng is no longer regarded as an authorized teacher of the Roman Catholic Church, Fr Schillebeeckx has been subjected to close cross-examination and Fr Boff, the leading South American theologian, had to agree not to publish in the immediate future. It is only a few years since the Modernist Oath (against the 'Syllabus of Errors') was withdrawn. At the same time this discipline against heresy is only exercised because it is the duty of the magisterium to keep the church's teaching consonant with the deposit of faith contained in scripture and tradition, rather than to tolerate accretions or deviations.

When we turn from the Roman Catholic Church to the Church of England, we find a more open – some would think too open – attitude to Anglican theologians and far less definition in Anglican formularies. The XXXIX Articles at first sight may seem rather negative, with Article VI asserting that scripture contains all things necessary to salvation and that nothing that cannot be found in or proved from scripture can be regarded as necessary. Article XXI seems to be negative about general councils, with its chief concern to affirm that they can err and they have erred, although the Article does admit that the findings of councils have authority when they are taken out of scripture (the first four ecumenical councils are specifically mentioned in the Act of Supremacy of 1559 and confirmed by the 1867 Lambeth Conference). Dr Emmanuel de Mendieta has pointed out the positive note of Article XX, in which it is asserted that the church has power to decree rites and ceremonies, and authority in controversies of faith, with the rider that, 'although the church is a witness and keeper of Holy Writ, yet, as it ought not to decree anything against the same, so besides the same ought it not to enforce anything to be believed for necessity of salvation'.[22] Furthermore, the Church of England accepts the Nicene Creed containing the word *homoousios* ('of one substance' with the Father) which is not a scriptural phrase but which correctly interprets scripture. It is not 'found in' scripture, nor 'proved by' scripture, but a valid interpretation of scripture. So tradition can include a valid interpretation of scripture; and in this sense there is here a doctrine of scripture, tradition and the teaching authority of the church consonant with that put forward in the Agreed Statement on Authority I.

But there is no explanation in the Articles about how the church should make pronouncements in matters of faith.

The Book of Common Prayer is also a source of doctrine for the Church of England, and here the unique nature of scripture can be seen not only in the regular reading of both Old and New Testaments, but also in the biblical language of the liturgy. Tradition too is reverenced not only by drawing on the liturgical riches of former ages, but also by the use of creeds in worship, a more frequent use than that of any other communion in Christendom. As for the teaching authority of the church, that too can be seen in the question asked of a bishop-designate at his consecration: 'Are you ready, with all faithful diligence, to banish and drive away all erroneous and strange doctrine contrary to God's word; and both privately and openly call upon others to do the same?'

The Canon Law of the Church of England has recently been revised, and its contents have been subjected to very rigorous synodical examination, and the new corpus has been promulged under special procedures to ensure that it expresses the mind of the Church of England. Canon A5 states:

> The doctrine of the Church of England is grounded in the Holy Scriptures and in such teachings of the ancient Fathers and Councils of the Church as are agreeable to the said Scriptures. In particular such doctrine is to be found in the Thirty-nine Articles of Religion, the Book of Common Prayer and the Ordinal.[23]

In addition, the oath of canonical obedience to a bishop, mentioned in Canon CI, testifies to the authority of a bishop in spiritual matters.[24]

Although there is no mention of it in Anglican formularies, it has been a tradition of the reformed Church of England to appeal to sound reason as a source of authority, to be combined with other sources of authority – sound reasoning about the Bible, as also about tradition. This can be seen particularly clearly in the writings of Hooker, the archetypal Anglican:

> The tradition and authority with which a man finds himself encompassed; the witness of his own heart and conscience recognizing and responding to the Spirit which meets him in the Bible; the scrutiny and appraising of the credentials which it offers to his reason; such is the threefold process which a man may use and which the Bible presupposes for the warrant of its claim to teach in God's Name, with His authority the means by which men now must reach the end for which they were created.[25]

The need for sound reasoning has become deeply embedded in the

Anglican ethos. Charles Gore, for example, believed in subjecting scripture to the rigours of critical examination, but he did so in the belief that the result would be the vindication of Catholic Christianity; and he was horrified at any falling away from the doctrine contained in the Nicene Creed. Unless reason is used under the guidance of Christian presuppositions, it ends in mere rationalism. Bishop Gore took fright at such a prospect and as a result of his agitation there was set up in 1922 a Commission to enquire into the nature and grounds of Christian doctrine. The Commission made its report in 1938 under its chairman William Temple. Significantly it was called *Doctrine in the Church of England*, not 'The Doctrine of the Church of England'. 'Our task has been, so far as we were able, to discuss the unchanging truths of the Christian revelation, and the various interpretations of these current in the Church of England, in such a way as to be intelligible to those of our contemporaries as have some acquaintance with theology.'[26] In this report symbolic acceptance of clauses in the creeds (including the virgin birth and the empty tomb) is accepted. In a note on assent it is said that general acceptance of the creeds does not necessarily mean assent to every phrase or proposition; but that if an authorized teacher puts forward personal opinions which diverge from the traditional teaching of the church, he must be careful to distinguish between such opinions and the normal teaching which he gives in the church's name; and so far as possible such divergences should be so put forward as to avoid offending consciences.[27] David Holloway has recently reminded us of the furore with which this liberalizing report was greeted, with a petition of protest signed by nearly half the clergy of the Church of England.[28]

However, the Second Great War intervened; and it was not until 1967 that a new Doctrine Commission was set up. Its first task was the preparation of a revised form of subscription to the formularies of the church, in view of the scruples of conscience that the current Declaration of Assent was causing ordinands, although it too had been earlier amended from its pristine form.[29] The new Declaration, preceded by a lengthy preface, is used not infrequently in the Church of England, and probably it provides the only occasion when a layman hears about the sources of authority for the Church of England:

The Church of England is part of the One, Holy, Catholic and

Apostolic Church, worshipping the one true God, Father, Son and Holy Spirit. It professes the faith uniquely revealed in the Holy Scriptures and set forth in the catholic creeds, which faith the Church is called upon to proclaim afresh in each generation. Led by the Holy Spirit, it has borne witness to Christian truth in its historic formularies, the Thirty-nine Articles of Religion, the Book of Common Prayer, and the Ordering of Bishops, Priest and Deacons. In the declaration you are about to make, will you affirm your loyalty to this inheritance of faith as your inspiration and guidance under God in bringing the grace and truth of Christ to this generation and making him known to those in your care?

This combines loyalty to the past unique revelation with the duty to 'proclaim afresh' the faith to the modern world. Professor Stephen Sykes has uncovered the ambiguity of this preface,[30] but without this ambiguity it is unlikely that the Commission, right at the start of its life, would have been able to produce a unanimous report. This became apparent some years later when the Doctrine Commission attempted to unpack the nature of the Christian faith and its expression in scriptures and creeds in its Report *Christian Believing*.[31] The fact that this report contains an agreed statement of 42 pages and a further 113 pages of individual essays, shows the difficulty that was experienced in finding consensus.

It may be noted that the Church of England's theologians are usually located in universities. (There was a time when I found myself the only parish priest on the Doctrine Commission.) In an age when secular winds blow through universities and when professors and lecturers may be separated from the regular worshipping life of the church, the appeal to sound reason, which is one of the excellencies of the Church of England, can easily degenerate into a critical and negative stance far removed from catholic Christianity. *Christian Believing* identified four attitudes to creeds:[32]

1. Creeds embody the standing truths of the gospel in the present as in the past.
2. Creeds express the general faith of the church although individuals may find difficulties over particular clauses.
3. Creeds can be neither affirmed nor denied, because more important than the past are fresh understandings of that continuing Christian enterprise which has its origins in Jesus.

4. Creeds deserve 'provisional' loyalty, but the essence of the Christian is found in a life of discipleship rather than credal affirmation.

With such diversity of views over creeds, the Roman Catholic Church might well ask whether there are any limits to the comprehensiveness of the Church of England! In fact a church can tolerate and even welcome very considerable diversity of belief, especially among its academic theologians, providing it has a firm base for its teaching authority. Presumably the Doctrine Commission, although accountable to General Synod, is part of the teaching authority of the Church of England. After the publication of the Report, all members of the Doctrine Commission except one were retired, which suggests that the teaching authority of this Commission was not recognized. A new Commission was appointed which produced a very different kind of report entitled *Believing in the Church*, with the subtitle 'The Corporate Nature of Faith'.[33] All the good things in this later report – and there were many – could not alter the fact that there exist within the Church of England respected theologians whose beliefs range from the ultra-traditional to the very radical.

One of the contributions to *Christian Believing* was concerned with unity and pluriformity in the New Testament. Professor Christopher Evans concluded that one of the chief results of New Testament criticism has been to show that the New Testament writings are frequently the result of a certain development and that they embody traditions that have been in development.[34] 'The movements may have been in the same direction, in parallel directions, or even in divergent directions.'[35] Nonetheless Professor Evans adds: 'This (pluralism) is not to be exaggerated. There is undoubtedly much common ground and unity of thought in the New Testament.'[36] The kind of divergence of view over the interpretation of creeds found among the authors of *Christian Believing* certainly cannot be vindicated by an appeal to pluralism in the New Testament.

Anglican comprehensiveness is sometimes justified on the grounds that it represents a *via media*, a mean between two extremes. Certainly moderation has played an important part in historic Anglicanism, in doctrine as well as in liturgy; and no doubt there were originally political reasons which made it expedient for

the Church of England to be equidistant between Calvinism and
Roman Catholicism. But the *via media* is not a principle that bears
much theological weight. *Via media* between what today? Even if
there is a fixed point at one end of the spectrum, there is not a
similar fixed point at the other! By way of contrast it is sometimes
said, after F. D. Maurice, that Anglicanism exists in a dynamic
tension between opposites. Once again, this concept does not bear
theological scrutiny. Professor Sykes is right in holding liberalism to
be parasitic, in the sense that it can only exist as a challenge to
traditional ways of thinking. *Ecclesia semper reformanda*, yes.
Doctrines must be restated in a new age with new thought forms.
But this is not to say that liberalism forms a 'party' within the church
that needs to be in creative tension with other ecclesastical 'parties'.

> Liberalism is a cuckoo in the Anglican nest, and the all-too facile
> inclusion of it under the guise of a 'party' with a long and
> honoured history in Anglicanism is bound to be no more than a
> temporary measure. If liberalism always has the instinct to
> challenge established authorities, no church which has once
> admitted that authorities can and should be interrogated will be
> able to devise an unchallengeable basis for itself. And this
> opinion may be *really opposed*, without any guarantee that all the
> expressed opinions are in some ineffable sense necessary to a
> higher truth. Persons in such a case will hold views which are
> contradictory of, not complementary to, those of other persons in
> the same church.[37]

A third way of interpreting the comprehensiveness of Anglicanism is to make a distinction between essential doctrine and
secondary doctrine. But it is difficult not merely to decide in which
category a particular doctrine falls, but also to show that essential
doctrines do continue unchanged from one language to another and
from one set of thought forms to another. Nonetheless this view of
essential and secondary doctrine has a long and honourable history
in Anglicanism,[38] and it has recently been re-stated by Professor
Root by speaking not of the Nicene Creed, but of the 'Nicene Faith'
as essential doctrine.[39] In that case the question may be put thus:
How must be the faith expressed today if the Nicene Fathers
expressed it as they did in their day?

Professor Sykes finds this interpretation open to the same
objection, namely, that essential doctrine could be held to change.

He prefers to find the source of Anglican doctrine in liturgical ethos and usage, and in the contents of liturgy, which are common to a particular church or province, and which its ordained ministers have promised to use. *Lex orandi, lex credendi* is an attractive principle. But he does not ask whether a doctrinal coherence exists within the Book of Common Prayer itself! Whereas liturgy undoubtedly influences the doctrinal position of a church, it does not control it. For all its problems, the explanation which makes use of essential doctrine and secondary doctrine has the most respectable history and is the most intellectually satisfying, and Anglicans should not be frightened of the idea of development – a concept which the ex-Anglican Cardinal Newman brought to the Roman Catholic Church – providing that Anglican doctrine is shaped by the Nicene Faith, and of course by its own historical past, as exemplified in the Thirty-nine Articles of Religion, the Book of Common Prayer and the Ordering of Bishops, Priests and Deacons. Here we can find a real and positive answer to the questions posed by the 1948 Lambeth Conference: 'Is Anglicanism based on a sufficiently coherent form of authority to form the nucleus of a world-wide fellowship of churches, or does its comprehensiveness conceal internal divisions which may cause its disruption?[40]

Certainly this kind of division between two kinds of doctrine does not solve all the problems of Anglican belief. Are secondary doctrines entirely dispensable? The Report *Doctrine in the Church of England* gives the impression that they are:

> The Commission is convinced that neither can the truth of the Gospel stand unimpaired, nor can any adequate account of its origin be given unless the broad tradition concerning Jesus, to which the Gospels and the Church have borne witness through the centuries, is accepted as historical, and in particular unless it is possible for the Church to proclaim that in the historical figure of Jesus of Nazareth 'the Word was made flesh and dwelt among us'.[41]

Such a position, however, is too broad. Anglicanism stands for more than incarnation. It is grounded in the triune God, and Christian faith itself is the gift of God about Christ through his Holy Spirit.

How then are lines to be drawn, if they have to be drawn? The Roman Catholic Church acts in a straight line, from scripture through tradition to its magisterium, although this is tempered by the principle of 'subsidiarity', namely that nothing ought to be done at a higher level than is necessary. Anglicanism by contrast functions less hierarchically, as indeed a recent Reith lecturer has suggested society itself now interacts. Anglicanism functions by means of a disseminated authority rather than 'line management', even if authority is chiefly mediated through the bishop as Father-in-God, 'wielding his authority in virtue of his divine commission and in synodical association with his clergy and laity, and exercising it in humble submission, as himself under authority'.

This concept of a disseminated authority was described in the Report of the 1948 Lambeth Conference:

> Catholic Christianity presents us with an organic process of life and thought in which religious experience has been, and is, described, intellectually ordered, mediated and verified. This experience is described in Scripture . . . It is defined in Creeds . . . It is mediated in the ministry of the Word and Sacraments . . . It is verified in the witness of the saints and in the *consensus fidelium* . . . This essentially Anglican authority is reflected in our adherence to episcopacy as the source of our order, and the Book of Common Prayer as the standard of our worship. Liturgy, in the sense of the offering and ordering of the public worship of God, is the crucible in which these elements of authority are fused and unified in the fellowship of power of the Holy Spirit.[42]

How have recent innovations affected the doctrine of the Church of England? Some people fear that the basis of authority for the Church of England has been changed with the passing of the Church of England (Worship and Doctrine) Measure 1974. This provides that any canon passed (by a two-thirds majority) under the measure shall have effect even if it is inconsistent with any of the rubrics of the Book of Common Prayer. It also provides that new forms of the Declaration of Assent to the doctrine of the Church of England can be made by canon (passed by a two-thirds majority) under the measure. Furthermore, it falls to the General Synod, under the measure, to decide whether any new canon, regulation, form of service or amendment is in accordance with the doctrine of the Church of England. There are safeguards (in what is known as Article 7 and Article 8 business) and the Convocations may exercise a delaying function, and there are rights reserved to the House of Bishops. Nonetheless, it appears to some that under these provisions the General Synod seems to have power to change the doctrine of the Church of England.

Any such changes declare the mind of the Church of England at the time when they are made rather than effect a permanent change in its doctrine. Without doubt General Synod has authority; but it is not the magisterium of the church in the sense in which Roman Catholics use that word. Canon A5 'Of the Doctrine of the Church of England' remains, whatever interpretation General Synod may give it; and the words of *Halsbury's Ecclesiastical Law*[43] must be born in mind:

> Synodical government is not to be interpreted as meaning that all the functions of Church government are concentrated in or subject to the General Synod; account must be taken not only of the royal supremacy, and of the ultimate legislative authority of Parliament, but also of the authority and powers exercised independently of the General Synod by the bishops, the ecclesiastical Courts and the Church Commissioners.

So Anglicanism, despite its apparent confusions, does contain within itself real sources of authority which enable it to formulate its essentials and to define the limits of Anglican belief, at least so far as its accredited preachers and clergy are concerned.

However, there are those who raise in this connection the subjection of the Church of England to Parliament. Cardinal Ratzinger, Prefect of the Roman Congregation of the Faith, writes about the Agreed Statements:

> Should one not also have gone into the question of the relation between political and ecclesiastical authority in the Church which first touches the nerve-point of the question of Catholicity of the Church or the relation between local and universal Church? In 1640 Parliament decided as follows: 'Convocation has no power to enact canons or constitutions concerning matters of doctrine or discipline, or in any other way to bind clergy or religious without the consent of Parliament.' That may be obsolete, but it came to my mind again in 1927 when on two occasions a version of the Book of Common Prayer was rejected by Parliament.[44]

These difficulties, if they be such, apply not to the Anglican Communion as a whole, but only to the Church of England. So far as worship is concerned, the Church of England now has power to devise alternative liturgies to those in the Book of Common Prayer, by means of the Worship and Doctrine Measure 1974, providing that these are theologically consonant with the Prayer Book. However, since Cardinal Ratzinger wrote that article, Parliament has turned down a further measure concerned with eradicating an outdated anomaly in the mandatory election by a Chapter of a bishop appointed by the Crown (although selected by the church). Ratzinger's point is a valid one. The Church of England cannot promulge new canons without the consent of Parliament, a matter on which Parliament itself is becoming increasingly sensitive. The parliamentary veto, originally intended as a safeguard for the laity, has become increasingly out of date with the advent of synodical government.

There are those who allege[45] that this restriction prevents the Church of England from qualifying as a church. Of course it does not, any more than governmental controls in e.g. USSR prevent the Russian Orthodox Church from being a church. If the parliamentary veto were to affect any vital part of the Church of England's life or doctrine, then the church should demand dis-establishment (and if this be refused, suffer as a Church under duress). The Church of England could still rightly claim to belong to the true and apostolic Church of Christ, as Canon AI claims.

But does the Roman Catholic Church accept this claim? According to Agreed Statement Authority in the Church II:

> The Second Vatican Council allows it to be said that a church out of communion with the Roman may lack nothing from the viewpoint of the Roman Catholic Church except that it does not belong to the visible manifestation of full Christian communion which is maintained in the Roman Catholic Church.[46]

Cardinal Ratzinger contradicts this claim,[47] and the Sacred Congregation for the Doctrine of the Faith asserts: 'According to Catholic tradition, visible unity is not something extrinsic added to particular churches, which already would possess and realize in themselves the full essence of the Church: this unity pertains to the intimate structure of faith.'[48] In support of it, the Agreed Statement refers to two passages from the Constitutions of Vatican II. The first, from the *Constitution on the Church*, reads:

The Church, constituted and organized in the world as a society, subsists in the Catholic Church, which is governed by the successor of Peter and by the bishops in union with that successor, although many elements of sanctification and truth can be found outside of her visible structure. These elements, however, as gifts properly belonging to the Church of Christ, possess an inner dynamism towards Catholic unity.[49]

Here it is not denied outright that a church out of communion with Rome may lack nothing except this full communion, but it is only actually stated that *many elements* of santification and of truth can be found within such a church. Similarly, after tracing the causes of schisms within the Great Church, the *Decree on Ecumenism* states:

As a result, many communions, national or denominational, were separated from the Roman See. Among those in which some Catholic traditions and institutions continue, the Anglican Communion occupies a special place.[50]

It could perhaps be said that 'some Catholic traditions and institutions' can be interpreted to mean 'all Catholic traditions and institutions except full communion with the Roman See', but that would be a strained interpretation.

In the *Decree on Ecumenism*, the 'separated brethren' are described as belonging to 'churches and ecclesial communities'. The Decree speaks freely of the Eastern churches as 'churches', but never uses the word 'church' of Anglicans, as though they are regarded as belonging not to churches but to ecclesial communities.

Maybe past history has made Anglicans unduly sensitive on this point. Certainly Pope Paul VI (as quoted in a footnote in Authority II)[51] spoke explicitly of the 'Anglican Church', and he looked forward to a time when the Roman Catholic Church 'is able to embrace her ever-beloved Sister in the one authentic communion of the family of Christ'. The point at issue, however, is more than a question about sensitivity; for the method adopted in the Agreed Statements, if it is to lead to a closer relationship, requires a mutual acceptance by Anglicans and Roman Catholics of their separated brethren as not merely displaying authentic *koinonia* but also as fellow members of the Catholic Church.

3

The Church and its
Structures of Authority

The first two Agreed Statements, the Windsor Statement of 1971 on Eucharistic Doctrine, and the Canterbury Statement of 1973 on Ministry and Ordination, when they are taken together with the Elucidations of Salisbury 1979, show a truly amazing convergence of doctrine between Rome and Canterbury. After so many centuries of controversy, it is uplifting to find that the Holy Spirit has guided the members of ARCIC to such a common mind. Their method of going behind past and present controversies to an understanding of the New Testament and the early church seems to have been fully justified. Their agreement is indeed 'substantial'. The only point at which the practice of the Roman Catholic Church and the Anglican Communion seems to differ sharply in these doctrinal areas is in connection with the reserved sacrament, whether or not adoration of Christ in the sacrament should be permitted (although the primary purpose of reservation is agreed by all to be sacramental reception). As ARCIC comments in its Eucharistic Doctrine: Elucidation, 'That there can be a divergence in matters of practice and in theological judgments relating to them, without destroying a common eucharistic faith, illustrates what we mean by *substantial* agreement.'[1] It is perhaps strange that there is no Agreed Statement on baptism (surely no divergence here?) and that nothing is said about the *number* of sacraments.

The Ministry and Ordination Elucidation ends with a section on Anglican orders. It claims that:

> our agreement on the essentials of eucharistic faith with regard to the sacramental presence of Christ and the sacrificial dimension of the eucharist, and on the nature and purpose of priesthood, ordination, and apostolic succession, is the new context in which the questions should now be discussed [concerning the mutual recognition of ministry]. This calls for a reappraisal of the verdict on Anglican Orders in *Apostolicae Curae* (1896).[2]

That statement was issued in 1979, and seven years have passed since then; and it is good to know that the Second Anglican-Roman Catholic International Commission (ARCIC II), recently set up, will be reviewing this question.

The story of the pronouncement against Anglican orders by Pope Leo XIII in *Apostolicae Curae* in 1896 and the events leading up to this, are told in considerable detail by the Roman Catholic writer J. J. Hughes.[3] The strong desire of Lord Halifax for a positive pronouncement as a step towards the reconciliation of the Church of England and the Roman Catholic Church becomes evident in the telling of the tale, as does the implacable hostility of Cardinal Vaughan to this objective, believing that it would bring harm to the Roman Catholic Church in England. Whether or not the papal decision was influenced by undue pressure from opponents such as Vaughan, it is not possible to say: *Apostolicae Curae* must be judged on its own merits. The Bull prudently omits the popular arguments (concerning valid succession) against the validity of Archbishop Parker's consecration,[4] none of which can be substantiated. It has three main points: first, that previous Popes had rejected Anglican orders and required those ordained under the Edwardine Ordinal to be ordained afresh; second, that the form of the sacrament ('Receive the Holy Ghost') was insufficient and third, that the intention also was insufficient, since all mention of the power to offer sacrifice had been removed from the rite. *Apostolicae Curae* was answered six months later by the response *Saepius Officio* of the Archbishops of Canterbury and York.[5] They had little difficulty in showing that Rome had in earlier days simply used 'Receive the Holy Ghost' as the form of the sacrament and that (apart from baptism, in which case the form of the sacrament was enjoined by Christ) no sacrament had a form fixed by a competent authority such as a general council. As for the intention of the Church of England in the ordination of priests and consecration of bishops, the Archbishops found it easy to show both from the Preface to the Ordinal and from the doctrine of eucharistic sacrifice contained within the Church of England's rite of holy communion (which only priests of course can celebrate), that the Church of England intends to continue the historic threefold order of the ordained ministry which the church has been given for the building up of the people of God. Fr Clark SJ, who had paid great attention to the circumstances surrounding the Bull, believes that, although there was indeed from the beginning an intention 'to do what the church does', there was also an overriding intention to exclude 'the power of the consecrating and sacrificing priesthood'.[6] The mass of evidence that he compiled about this matter has, however, been interpreted very differently by others, both Roman Catholics and Anglicans, who believe that the English Reformers were justified in their attack on the mass and on the eucharistic theology of the time, and that it was perfectly possible to combine this with a sincere desire to simplify and purify the rites conferring the historic orders of the catholic church.[7]

Hughes, in asking for a reappraisal of the question, notes that 'hitherto most catholic writing about Anglican orders has been characterized by a desire to see how much could be said against the orders, not how much could be said for them. The result of all such studies is a foregone conclusion.'[8] Now that Roman Catholic and Anglican theologians, official members of an official Anglican-Roman Catholic International Commission, are able to be in substantial agreement both about eucharistic doctrine and about ministry and ordination, it would seem desirable, if Anglicans are to be assured of the continuing goodwill of the Roman Catholic Church in their joint undertaking, that such a reappraisal should speedily be accomplished by ARCIC II, or by some other body set up for this purpose. The Ministry and Ordination Elucidation closed with these words:

> Mutual recognition presupposes acceptance of the apostolicity of each other's ministry. The Commission believes that its agreements have demonstrated a consensus in faith on eucharist and ministry which has brought closer the possibility of such acceptance. It hopes that its own conviction will be shared by members

of both our communions; but mutual recognition can only be achieved by the decision of our authorities. It has been our mandate to offer to them the basis upon which they may make this decision.[9]

Without this reappraisal of the validity of Anglican orders, and so long as the official Roman Catholic judgment holds that they are 'absolutely null and utterly void', it seems improbable that any real progress towards organic unity can be achieved. Fortunately, ARCIC II will be taking on board this reappraisal, and Cardinal Jan Willebrandts, President of the Roman Catholic Secretariat for Fostering Christian Unity, has written, in a letter to the co-chairmen of ARCIC II dated 13 July 1985, with reference to the Agreed Statements on the Eucharist and on Ordination that 'the explicit profession of one faith in Eucharist and Ministry, together with the possible effects of such a profession on the Roman Catholic Church's evaluation of the Anglican formularies of ordination would be the strongest possible stimulus to find ways to overcome the difficulties which still hinder a mutual recognition of ministries, those hindrances which ARCIC II is commissioned to study.' This is a coded statement suggesting the possible super-session of *Apostolicae Curae*. (Unfortunately, if mutual acceptance of these Agreed Statements leads towards a closer relationship between the two churches, the Anglican Church Society [an Evangelical body] has announced its intention to bring about a schism in the Church of England, speaking darkly of a 'continuing Church'.)

Priests and bishops validly ordained play an important part in the life of the church in building it up in faith and hope and love, and acting as shepherds to the flock of Christ. In the previous chapter, those who bear high office in the church were considered in so far as they constitute a *source* of authority. In this chapter they will be considered in connection with the *exercise* of authority through the formal structure of the church, although the two aspects of authority are of course interconnected.

The Agreed Statement Authority in the Church I recognizes that God raises up certain individuals with special gifts which entitle them to speak and to be heeded.[10] Those who have ministerial authority come under the oversight of the bishop, who has chief pastoral authority. The Statement recognizes that:

The authorities in the Church cannot adequately reflect Christ's authority because they are still subject to the limitations and sinfulness of human nature. Awareness of this inadequacy is a continual summons to reform.[11]

The Statement also recognizes that churches in a region group themselves together under the leadership of a bishop of a principal see within the region as a sign of co-responsibility and as a form of episcopal collegiality. These may be bishops, patriarchs or primates or chairmen of episcopal conferences.

This 'ideal' structure appears to give a coherent structure of authority within the church within a region.

How does it compare to the actual situation in the Roman Catholic Church? According to the *Dogmatic Constitution on the Church*:

This sacred Synod teaches that by divine institution bishops have succeeded to the place of the apostles as shepherds of the Church, and he who hears them hears Christ, while he who rejects them rejects Christ and Him who sent Christ.[12]

This appears to represent a somewhat higher doctrine of the episcopate than that found in the Agreed Statements. According to the same Constitution, 'episcopal consecration, together with the office of sanctifying, also confers the offices of teaching and governing'.[13] So far as priests are concerned, they are to be 'prudent co-operators with the episcopal order'[14]. The Constitution also makes room for uniate churches, churches which 'have in the course of time coalesced into several groups, organically united, which, preserving the unity of faith and the unique constitution of the universal Church, enjoy their own discipline, their own liturgical usage, and their own theological and spiritual heritage'.[15] This passage is of particular interest to the Anglican Communion, for it describes what might be a possible relationship between Canterbury and Rome in a somewhat modified church.

Bishops are said to govern the particular churches entrusted to them as the vicars and ambassadors of Christ.[16] Here again the doctrine seems somewhat more advanced than that of the Agreed Statement, for there at least there is no confusion with the invisible head of the church and his visible representatives, as the phrase 'vicars of Christ' unfortunately implies. The power which bishops exercise is said to be 'proper, ordinary and immediate'; and indeed without such power, they could hardly govern their dioceses, although of course it must be exercised with humility after the example of the Good Shepherd. Bishops are bishops in their own right, and not mere delegates of a higher human authority. The Constitution further recognizes that from early times there were established regional synods and provincial councils of bishops, so that resources could be pooled and plans unified for the common good and for the strengthening of individual churches.[17] Accordingly, episcopal conferences were decreed as a kind of council in which the bishops of a given nation or territory jointly exercise their pastoral office in matters of common concern. An episcopal conference will draft its own statutes, and is empowered to make decisions (to be ratified by higher authority) by two-thirds majority. Episcopal conferences may be established by bishops of different nations if special circumstances require. From this short resumé of episcopal authority there seems to be substantial agreement between Roman Catholic doctrine and the Agreed Statements, except that in the latter a bishop is not given the authority of the vicar of Christ.

What is the Anglican view of these matters? Cardinal Ratzinger writes in this connection:

Any presentation of the theme 'Authority in the Church' which was really intended to lead to unity, would have to take into account in a much more concrete way the actual form of authority in order to do justice to the question. For if there was surprise afterwards at the fact that the Roman Catholic Church can give an authoritative answer more immediately than Anglican structures allow for, this is surely an indication that too little attention has been paid to the actual functioning of authority . . . The text left one completely in the dark as to the concrete structure of authority in the Anglican community. Those well acquainted with Anglicanism know that the Lambeth Conference, originally instituted in 1867, was not due to meet for several years, according to its regular timing, and that no authoritative pronouncement could be made before that date. But ought not the text to have mentioned this structure in order to give a true explanation of the nature of authority without stopping short of this concrete reality? Would not the right and necessary thing to have been to explain what sort of teaching authority does or does not belong to this assembly of bishops?[18]

It is necessary to give this long quotation, because of the importance of this comment by the Prefect of the Roman Catholic Congregation of the Faith, even though he writes in a private capacity. The importance of this comment is twofold. In the first place, it implies a rejection of the whole method of ARCIC, and secondly it implies an ignorance of the Anglican Communion.

It was the intention of ARCIC to produce 'the ideal of the church as willed by Christ', as the co-chairmen's Preface to Authority in the Church I put it, rather than 'to pay attention to the actual functioning authority' as Cardinal Ratzinger asks. But Cardinal Ratzinger regards it as unsatisfactory to stop at the end of the first millenium, however satisfactory a method this may have seemed when the Roman Catholic Church was dealing with the Orthodox churches:

> For this way of looking at it actually implies denials of the existence of the Universal Church in the second millenium, while tradition as a living, truth-giving power is frozen at the end of the first. This strikes at the very heart of the idea of Church and tradition, because ultimately such an age test dissolves the full authority of the Church, which is then left without a voice in the present day. Moreover one might well ask in reply to such an assertion, with what right consciences, in such a particular Church as the Latin Church would then be, could be bound by such pronouncements. What once appeared as truth would have to be reduced to mere custom. The great age-long claim to truth would be disqualified as an abuse.[19]

It lies with Roman Catholics rather than to Anglicans to respond to this criticism; and it may not be easy for them to do so. One cannot help feeling some sympathy with the Cardinal when he writes: 'Ecumenical dialogue does not mean opting out of living, Christian reality but advancing by means of the hermeneutics of unity.'[20]

A second comment must be made on Cardinal Ratzinger's request 'to pay attention to the actual functioning authority of Anglicanism'. He is under a misapprehension if he believes that a Lambeth Conference can speak authoritatively for the whole Anglican Communion. The Lambeth Conference, as its name implies, is a conference, not a synod with legislative powers. The Roman Catholic Church, predominantly Western in ethos if not in membership, understands church government primarily in legislative terms, although Vatican II made a welcome shift towards a more pastoral concern. The Anglican Communion, after trials and tribulations in church courts and secular courts in England during the last century, prefers to work through consultation and persuasion, although it has some disciplinary powers in reserve. The churches and provinces represented by the Lambeth Fathers are under no legal obligation to carry out resolutions passed at a Lambeth Conference, although there belongs to such resolutions the spiritual authority that is proper to a conclave of all the Fathers-in-God of the Communion. But it must be said that Lambeth resolutions are passed without the assistance of the clergy and laity of the church; and although the bishops of the Church of England have a special responsibility for teaching and for governing the church, they act with full authority only as bishops-in-synod, rather than as bishops on their own, in the same kind of way as (in accordance with Roman Catholic teaching) the Pope's authority is fully expressed in union with his fellow bishops.

In the Anglican Communion a bishop is owed obedience by his clergy in all things lawful and right, and at his consecration he is exhorted:

> Be to the flock of Christ a shepherd, not a wolf; feed them, devour them not. Hold up the weak, heal the sick, bind up the broken, bring again the outcasts, seek the lost. Be so merciful, that you be not too remiss; so minister discipline, that you forget not mercy: that when the chief Shepherd shall appear you may receive the never-fading crown of glory.

In addition to the duty of governing, the bishop also has the task of teaching. He is told to 'give heed to reading, exhortation, and doctrine. Think upon the things contained in this book (the Bible) . . . Take heed unto thyself and to doctrine, and be diligent in doing them.'

Anglican bishops gather together in episcopal synods by provinces (or in the case of the Church of England, usually Canterbury jointly with York). National churches tend to have national episcopal councils. The degree of authority given to these episcopal councils differs in different provinces. Some have certain matters reserved to them, some have a general power of veto. Some provincial synods began as bishops' conferences and have retained a House of Bishops as a kind of upper chamber with the right to approve the work of a lower house. In some conferences the Primate has the right to visit and to supervise individual dioceses, and in others there is a joint primacy of all bishops in the conference, with one of them chosen to act as chairman. It is a characteristic of the Anglican Communion that provincial constitutions have grown up by local custom rather than imposed hierarchically from above.

Provincial government is more than a democratic system of checks and balances. It is embodiment of the principle of diversified authority spelt out at the first Lambeth Conference – common concerns are Provincial concerns: local problems require local initiatives. Again balance differs from Province to Province and this partly reflects the circumstances in which Provinces are founded. If a Province came into being through the sub-division of a large unit, its provincial authority will tend to be centralized; if it is an amalgamation of previously existing churches, then its structure is bound to be of a more federal character.[21]

What authority on matters of doctrine do these provincial or national meetings of Anglican bishops possess? Here to some extent we are sailing on uncharted waters, because – at least in the Church of England – synodical government is still a tender plant of some fifteen years of age. However, the controversy in the Church of England brought about by the remarks made by Dr David Jenkins when Bishop-designate of Durham and by the decision of the Archbishop of York to proceed with his consecration, is instructive. The bishops as a consequence have been asked to produce a statement of belief, with special reference to the virginal conception of Jesus and his physical resurrection. This statement has been presented to General Synod, with its three Houses of Bishops, Clergy and Laity. It is possible (but unknown at the time of writing) that the bishops will wish to take back their statement and amend it in the light of this debate. What is clear, however, is that the bishops have a special responsibility for teaching (both in commending the faith to others and in preserving it from error) but that this responsibility should be exercised in synod, in consultation with both laity and clergy.

The Agreed Statement moves on from consideration of episcopal authority to consider conciliar and primatial authority. According to Authority in the Church I it is by this means that local churches are kept faithful in universal communion to achieve the embodiment of that unity for which Christ prayed.[22]

Councils have played a vital part in clarifying and protecting the Church's faith; and this is recognized in the Agreed Statements on Authority in the Church. However, the criteria by which a council is regarded as ecumenical still need definition.[23] The authority which is rightly given to these councils is circumscribed by the need for their decisions to have been founded in scripture and consonant with tradition, and by the recognition that categories of thought and modes of expression used in some authoritative statement may become outmoded, so that subsequent restatement is necessary.[24]

Authority in the Church I affirms that when the church meets in ecumenical council about fundamental matters of faith, its judgments, providing that they are faithful to scripture and consistent with tradition, are protected from error by the Holy Spirit;[25] and this doctrine is further explained in the Elucidation.[26] What is not stated, however, is the authority for such a view about ecumenical councils. Preservation from error is not promised in the holy scripture to any person or group of persons. 'The Holy Spirit will guide you into all truth' (John 16.13), certainly; but that is an argument for the indefectibility of the church, in the sense that it will not persist in error, rather than an argument for the preservation from error of an ecumenical council. More evidence for and explanation of this claim to preservation from error seems to be needed before it can be accepted as well founded.

The Agreed Statements on Authority affirm the need of a universal primate, on the grounds that the unity of the church needs universal visible expression, and that the maintenance of that visible unity at the universal level includes the *episcope* of a universal primate as well as universal conciliarity; and since a claim to this universal primacy has emerged in the see of Rome, and has been recognized by the majority of Christendom, there is a strong presumption that this has come about through the guidance of the Holy Spirit. (There is, it is said, no simple transfer of Peter's authority to his followers.) As the Faith and Order Advisory Group of the General Synod has pointed out, it is not clear whether and to what extent a need for universal *episcope* includes the exercise of oversight by a single person; and appeals to the working of divine providence in history are open to more than one interpretation.[27] Furthermore, the same group questions here the argument from history, in view of the admission that Popes have not always lived up to the requirements of their sacred office. The Statement speaks in terms of the ideal, not the actual; and 'if a description of an actual development is regarded as providential, then that development and not some similar but distinct ideal ought to become prescriptive'.[28] The group remarks that arguments for a providential provision of this kind appear readily more compelling to those who already possess the ministry in question, whether it be episcopacy or papacy, than to those who do not. This is a two-edged remark; for Anglicans who have been given in episcopacy a sign of unity and an instrument for the church's wholeness might by the same token be expected to accept these at the universal level in the office of a universal primate.

The universal primate is said to act in union with the bishops throughout. Although they hold their episcopate in their own right, at the same time they always exercise it in union with the universal primate. Authority in the Church II states:

> The Church's decision is normally given through synodical decision, but at times a primate acting in communion with his fellow bishops may articulate the decision even apart from a synod. Although responsibility for preserving the Church from fundamental error belongs to the whole Church, it may be exercised on its behalf by a universal primate.[29]

Once again, the question must be pressed about the grounds for believing that the church, in any one particular decision, will be preserved from error by the Holy Spirit of God, even if the decision is based upon scripture; for no promise of infallibility is given in scripture, and even though we place a very high authority on the words of scripture, in default of a claim to infallibility, it is not easy to see how we can properly make that claim on behalf of scripture.

Primacy and conciliarity are said in the Agreed Statements to be complementary elements of *episcope*; but it is not stated how there could be any councils at all unless they were summoned by the universal primate (in the same kind of way as *mutatis mutandis* the

Archbishop of Canterbury invites bishops to the Lambeth Conference.) A universal primate who was merely a 'constitutional monarch' would hardly give the church direction; yet one who gave positive leadership in a particular direction might be unacceptable. Cardinal Ratzinger points out that originally the authority of the emperor was necessary to summon a council, but that in the process of history the Athanasian concept of the church prevailed over the Eusebian, and the function of summoning a council devolved on the bishop of Rome.[30] In any case the days when the church might look to a 'godly prince' have passed. Could there be any other valid way of summoning a council? And if not, could it be said (as the Response of the Roman Catholic Bishop's Conference of England and Wales suggests) that the Agreed Statements give insufficient weight to the universal primacy as intrinsic to the nature of the Church?[31]

In any case it is not entirely clear in what the complementarity of primacy and conciliarity is thought to consist. Presumably what is meant is that the whole Christian community cannot be united in faith and love without both conciliar and primatial *episcope*: yet nonetheless there are occasions when primatial authority may be used on behalf of the whole church without invoking conciliar authority as well. Presumably this is equivalent to saying, at a different level, that the proper way of uniting a diocese in faith and love is through the bishop-in-synod, but there are many occasions when the bishop has to act on his own initiative.

This is the ideal picture of universal primate put forward in the two Agreed Statements on Authority. The claim of the universal primate to be acting *de jure divino* is explained by the emergence of the papal office in the course of history by divine providence. How satisfactory is such an explanation? Providence may express only the permissive will of God, while *de jure divino* seems rather to express the deliberate intention of God to guard and guide his church. It might be proved to be *de jure divino* by revelation, but not simply by the fact of its development. As for the attribution of universal, ordinary and immediate jurisdiction to the universal primate, this would seem to be paralleled by the duty of a bishop to exercise his jurisdiction at parish level (through inhibition or by other means) if the pastoral situation demands, in order to preserve the faith and unity of the people of God in a parish at a time of pastoral crisis. It is made clear that the universal primate must exercise his jurisdiction under moral limits in order to safeguard the faith and unity of the universal church: this is not an autocratic power but a service exercised in collegial association by the primate with his fellow bishops.[32]

Such is the ideal picture put forward by ARCIC. It differs in some important respects from the actual exercise of papal power, as well as from the picture of the bishops, councils and papacy expressed in the Vatican II documents. There it is said:

> The college of the body of bishops has no authority unless it is simultaneously conceived of in terms of its head, the Roman Pontiff, Peter's successor, and without any lessening of his power of primacy over all, pastors as well as the general faithful. For in virtue of his office, that is, as Vicar of Christ and pastor of the whole Church, the Roman Pontiff has full, supreme and universal power over the Church. And he can always exercise this power freely.[33]

No mention here of moral limits, and the Pontiff's power is said to be 'full, supreme' without any mention of the college of bishops with whom and on behalf of whom he exercises it. The Pontiff also is called 'the Vicar of Christ', as though he is set apart on earth to take the place of Christ. Yet the Lord Jesus Christ took a little child, put his arm round him and said, 'whoever receives one of these children in my name receives me' (Mark 9.37). The Archbishops remarked in their response to *Apostolicae Curae*: 'That error, which is inveterate in the Roman Communion, of substituting the visible head for the invisible Christ will rob the good words of our brother, the Pope, of any fruit of peace.' Today we would not wish to use such language. But we dare not pass over the point.

The *Dogmatic Constitution on the Church* further describes the relationship of the Pope and his episcopate:

> The order of bishops is the successor to the college of the apostles in teaching authority and pastoral rule; or rather in the episcopal order the apostolic body continues without a break. Together with its head, the Roman Pontiff, and never without this head, the episcopal order is the subject of supreme and full power over the universal church. But this power can be exercised only with the consent of the Roman Pontiff.[34]

It is not clear how this 'full and supreme power' can inhere both in the college of bishops and in the Supreme Pontiff, unless it is intended to signify that it inheres in the Supreme Pontiff in union with the college of bishops; but in that case it is not easy to account for the previous excerpt, which seems to attribute this full and supreme power to him alone, unless the latter has been included merely because of the earlier definition on papal infallibility at the First Vatican Council in 1870:

> The Roman Pontiff, when he speaks *ex cathedra* (that is, when fulfilling the office of Pastor and Teacher of all Christians on his supreme apostolical authority he defines a doctrine concerning faith or morals to be held by the Universal Church) through the divine assistance promised him in blessed Peter, is endowed with that infallibility, with which the Divine Redeemer has willed that his Church – in defining doctrine concerning faith or morals – should be equipped: and, therefore that such definitions of the Roman Pontiff of themselves – and not by virtue of the consent of the Church – are irreformable. If any one shall presume (which God forbid!) to contradict this our definition; let him be anathema!

There are several points here which differ from the Agreed Statement. In the first place, the Roman Pontiff is said to have been promised assistance by the 'blessed Peter', but in the Agreed Statement Authority in the Church II it is said that the New Testament contains no explicit record of a transference of Peter's leadership; nor is the transmission of apostolic authority in general very clear.[35] The Bishops of England and Wales question whether this way of handling the Petrine texts gives sufficient weight to the 'lived tradition of the Catholic Church'.[36] Secondly in the Vatican I Definition there is a mention of both faith and morals, whereas the Agreed Statements make mention only of statements to preserve 'faith and unity'. In general the Definition of Vatican I and the *Dogmatic Constitution on the Church* of Vatican II seem to advance the office of the Supreme Pontiff far beyond 'the sign of the visible *koinonia* God wills for his Church and an instrument through which unity in diversity is realized',[37] which is how a universal primate is envisaged in the Agreed Statement Authority in the Church II.

Furthermore, in the *Dogmatic Constitution on the Church*, the authority of the words of bishops, and in particular those of the Supreme Pontiff, are to be regarded with far more awe and respect, even when the latter is not speaking *ex cathedra*, than seems to be envisaged in the Agreed Statements:

> Bishops, teaching in communion with the Roman Pontiff, are to be respected by all as witnesses to divine and Catholic truth. In matters of faith and morals, the bishops speak in the name of Christ and the faithful are to accept their teaching and adhere to it with a religious assent of soul. This religious submission of will and of mind must be shown in a special way to the authentic teaching of the Roman Pontiff, even when he is not speaking *ex cathedra*. That is, it must be shown in such a way that his supreme magisterium is acknowledged with reverence, the judgments made by him are sincerely adhered to, according to his manifest mind and will. His mind and will in the matter may be known chiefly either from the character of the documents, or from his manner of speaking.[38]

The respect to be shown to bishops here, and in particular to the Roman Pontiff, is alien to the ethos of Anglicanism. The point is well put by the Report of the Faith and Order Advisory Group:

> The absence from Anglican experience for more than four hundred years of a universal primacy invested with even a qualified and conditional sovereignty in teaching and in jurisdiction makes Anglicans inclined to understand decision-making by authority in terms of a developing dialogue, including criticism and response, rather than as a monologue. We should have welcomed it if ARCIC had been able to say something about the openness of authority to constructive criticism . . . Anglicans, while they are aware of the Lord's warning against offending the weak (Matt. 18.6) naturally think that it is often the duty of authority not to bring debate to a speedy conclusion but rather to ensure that legitimate options are kept open or even protected.[39]

Anglicans have no experience of councils in which it is claimed that pronouncements are kept free from error by the guidance of the Holy Spirit; and while Anglican bishops act in concert with their fellow bishops, with due deference to the metropolitical rights of their Primate, they regard him as *primus inter pares* whose pronouncements are to be treated with respect, but to whom it is not fitting to give submission of mind or will. (Such submission does not, however, seem to be expected in the Agreed Statements.) Anglicans recognize that it is useful for Primates to consult together, as they do from time to time in Primates' Meetings; but they also recognize the importance of representative bishops, clergy and laity consulting together, as they do in the Anglican Consultative Council, which has no counterpart in the meetings to represent the universal church envisaged in the Agreed Statements.

While a movement from the actual situation in the Roman Catholic Church today to the 'ideal' envisaged in the Agreed Statements would need some major changes of ethos as well as of practice for Roman Catholics, so far as Anglicans are concerned, the changes needed would be greater. They would, I think, find it very difficult to ascribe total freedom from error (by divine guidance) to any considered Statement by a universal primate or by conciliar authority, even though it were granted that the teaching authority of the church has no power to create new truths or to add to the faith. Even if they could agree to the immediate universal jurisdiction of a universal primate, they would, I think, require the moral and spiritual limits of this jurisdiction to be fully defined. They would also, I think, agree that 'consideration of universal oversight should be developed in closer connection with an emphasis on the right and sometimes duty of the community to engage in critical discussion of decisions on faith and morals'.[40] And I think that the kind of diversity which was remarked on in the New Testament by Professor Christopher Evans' contribution to *Christian Believing*[41] should not only be tolerated but actively encouraged within the church, in the belief that truth is best articulated by free questioning as much as by listening, and by the use of critical faculties as much as by appropriate submission.

Two further questions must be asked by Anglicans. The first concerns their own integrity. Would acceptance of the 'ideal' envisaged in the Agreed Statements mean that they would have admitted that before the reconciliation of the Anglican Communion with the Roman Catholic Church, Anglicanism lacked something that made it a church? The Agreed Statements make it clear that, in the judgment of ARCIC, this is not the case. 'Being in canonical communion with the Bishop of Rome is not among the necessary elements by which a Christian community is recognized as a church.'[42] It must, however, be noted with sadness that Cardinal Ratzinger contradicts this statement.[43] If this could be agreed, then both the Anglican Communion and the Roman Catholics would through reunion be greatly enriched by what they each lack on account of the schism between the two communions. Roman Catholics 'would be enriched by the presence of a particular tradition of spirituality and scholarship . . . and by involving the laity in the life and mission of the church,'[44] and Anglicans would be vastly enriched also by being reconciled to the largest church in Christendom from whom sadly they were cut off in 1570, just over four hundred years ago, by the Bull *Regnans in Excelsis*.

The second question that must be asked is whether by accepting the 'ideal' set forth in the Agreed Statements Anglicans are implying that they were wrong to go into schism with the Roman Catholic Church. If the unity in truth of the visible church needs visible expression, and if maintenance of that visible unity at the universal level includes the *episcope* of a universal primate, and that primate is located in the see of Rome, could the Church of England ever have been justified in remaining in schism as a result of *Regnans in Excelsis*? Should not the result of the Bull have been to make the Church of England return to communion with the Bishop of Rome?

The Agreed Statements represent an 'ideal' picture of the authority of the church. It is generally agreed that the realities of the situation on both sides were very far from ideal. Political motives were mixed up with religious convictions. Reconciliation means mutual acceptance without trying to apportion blame for the past. The vision that beckons the Anglican Church is of a reconciled and reunited church, maintaining its integrity from the past, and sharing in love and faith in union with those from who it is now so sadly separated.

4

The Church and the Laity

The laity have not been mentioned so far in this discussion about future relationships between the Anglican Communion and the Roman Catholic Church. This is not because of their unimportance. On the contrary, as Kathleen Bliss wrote over twenty years ago,[1] at least 99.5% of the church is lay, despite the fact that 'going into the church' is common parlance for being ordained. In fact the subject is so important that it deserves a chapter to itself.

As Dr Henry Chadwick has reminded us,[2] the Agreed Statement Authority in the Church I clearly states that 'the perception of God's will for his church does not belong only to the ordained ministry but is shared by all its members'.[3] Nonetheless, elsewhere in the Agreed Statement this perception is understood by way of response rather than initiative. This need not necessarily be its exclusive meaning, but it seems to be the only one mentioned in the Agreed Statement. 'The community must for its part respond to and assess the insights and teaching of the ordained ministers.'[4] In the Elucidation ARCIC spells out what is meant by 'reception'. 'By "reception" we mean the fact that the people of God acknowledge such a decision or statement because they recognize in it the apostolic faith. They accept it because they discern a harmony between what is proposed to them and the *sensus fidelium* of the whole Church . . . . Reception does not create truth nor legitimize the decision; it is the final indication that such a decision has fulfilled the necessary conditions for it to be a true expression of the faith.'[5]

Members of ARCIC further defend themselves from the charge that they have neglected the laity. They emphasize that every member of the church has a role to play. They even claim that the Roman Catholic Church has sought to integrate into decision-making those who are not ordained, although it would seem that this role is one of ratification rather than decision-taking. ARCIC members maintain that the reason why they have given so much space to the ordained ministry (and by contrast so little space to the laity) is that the former is the area where most difficulties exist, and that this in no way devalues the proper and active role of the laity.

ARCIC returns to this subject once more in Authority in the Church II while discussing the guaranteed gift of divine assistance in freedom from error attached to the Bishop of Rome by virtue of his formal decisions. ARCIC points out that Anglicans (if indeed they can ever accept that this gift exists) would require reception by the faithful before they could acknowledge that any such pronouncement was free from error. ARCIC comments:

> The problem about reception is inherently difficult. It would be incorrect to suggest that in controversies of faith no conciliar or papal definition possesses a right to attentive sympathy and acceptance until it has been examined by every individual Christian and subjected to the scrutiny of his private judgment.[6]

Reception is indeed a thorny subject. It is by no means impossible that positive reception in one era might be followed by a less positive reception in the following era (e.g. in connection with the Marian dogmas). Just what does reception mean – unanimous approval, or approval by the majority, and if the latter, how is that majority to be ascertained? To some at least it might seem that the attempt to rationalize the dogma of infallibility is beset with overwhelming difficulties.

The question that must be asked is whether this account of the laity does full justice to the role which lay people should be expected to play in the church today, and whether it does full justice to the role which they played in New Testament times. Certainly Paul spoke with the authority of an apostle, and he does not seem to have expected more than 'reception' for his pronouncements from the churches in his sphere of influence and authority. In dealing with his judgment on a man who has committed incest with his mother-in-law, Paul wrote: 'Though I am absent in body, I am present in spirit and my judgment upon the man who did this thing is already given as if I were indeed present: you all being assembled together in the name of our Lord Jesus, and I with you in spirit, with the power of our Lord Jesus Christ, this man is to be consigned to Satan . . .' (I Cor. 5.3). Paul seems to make his own judgment here without the consent of the congregation; but this is not perhaps a straightforward case, since Paul was not present with the congregation and could hardly make his judgment together with them.

A more straightforward instance is the Council in Jerusalem as recounted in Acts 15. Certainly James is said to have begun his summing up with the words: 'My judgment is . . .', but we are told that 'the apostles and elders, with the agreement of the whole church, resolved to choose representatives and to send them to Antioch; and the letter that they were to deliver contained the phrase: 'It is the decision of the Holy Spirit, and our decision . . .' (v. 28). The apostles certainly took the initiative; but the elders and the people took a more active part than mere reception, and themselves participated in the decision-taking process. In those early days, of course, there was no clear distinction between lay people and ordained, at least so far as the presbyterate was concerned; but nonetheless the distinctions made in the text between apostles, elders and the whole church in some ways correspond to today's distinction between bishops, priests and lay people. In general it can be said with confidence about the New Testament that, while the apostles speak with special authority as receiving their commission from Christ himself (apart from Matthias), there is nothing to suggest that the role of the ordinary Christian in decision-taking is confined to reception.

The role of the laity as set out in the Agreed Statements follows quite closely the role attributed to lay people in the Roman Catholic Church.

Considerable attention is paid to the laity in the Documents of Vatican II, both in the *Dogmatic Constitution on the Church* and also in the *Decree on the Apostolate of the Laity*. Lay persons are of course incorporated into the royal priesthood and holy people that they may offer spiritual sacrifices through everything they do and may witness to Christ throughout the world.[7] Although they have 'the capacity to be deputed by the hierarchy to exercise certain church functions for a spiritual purpose',[8] by and large the role of the lay people, as envisaged in the Roman Catholic Church, is to glorify God by witnessing to his kingdom in the secular world, and by offering their secular work to God and thereby consecrating it; and they should also use every opportunity to commend the gospel of Jesus Christ by the quality of their lives and by more direct evangelism in the secular world. The job of the priests and bishops is to run the church and to decide doctrine and to administer sacraments; the job of the lay person, nourished by the grace of the sacraments and other means of grace, is to glorify God in his world, to consecrate the world of home and work, and to win people for Christ in his church. The division is simple, and clearly understood. The various Vatican II documents expand on this theme.

The role of the layman is set out in the *Dogmatic Constitution on the Church*:

> A secular quality is proper and special to laymen . . . The laity by their very vocation seek the Kingdom of God by engaging in secular affairs and by ordering them according to the will of God. They live in the world, that is, in each and in all of the secular professions and occupations. They live in the ordinary circumstances of family and social life, from which the very web of their existence is woven. They are called there by God so that, by exercising their proper function and being led by the spirit of the Gospel they can work for the sanctification of the world from within, in the manner of leaven. In this way they can make Christ known to others, especially by the testimony of a life resplendent in faith, hope and charity. The layman is closely involved in secular affairs of every kind. It is therefore his special task to illumine and organize these affairs in such a way that they may always start out, develop and persist according to Christ's mind, to the praise of the Creator and the Redeemer.[9]

The next section makes plain the contrast between laymen and priests:

> They also have for their brothers in the sacred ministry those who by teaching, by sanctifying and by ruling with the authority of Christ, so feed the family of God that the new commandment of charity may be fulfilled by all.[10]

Lay people are free to undertake various forms of lay apostolate by their own free choice; but no project 'may claim the name "Catholic" unless it has obtained the consent of the lawful Church authority'. A short reference is made to more spiritual tasks to be undertaken by laity:

> The hierarchy entrusts to the laity some functions which are more closely connected with pastoral duties, such as the teaching of Christian doctrine, certain liturgical actions and the care of souls. By virtue of this mission, the laity are fully subject to ecclesiastical direction in the performance of their work.[11]

It is strange that this matter occupies so short a space in the Decree. Twenty years later, lay ecclesial ministries still only receive a passing mention in the Consultation Document *Ex Ecclesiae Coetibus* prepared in advance of the meeting of the International Synod of Bishops in October 1986 on the theme of the laity. After quoting from the Apostolic Exhortation *Evangelii Nuntiandi* of Paul VI, the document adds:

> The experience which in recent years some local churches have passed through urges renewed reflection on the ministries entrusted to the laity. Such reflection cannot avoid considering attentively the true nature both of the ecclesial 'ministry' in general, and, in particular, the ecclesial distinctiveness of the laity, especially their 'secular' condition. It is necessary to bear in mind that the term ministries is sometimes used with a varying range of meaning (26).

This somewhat obscure language is odd in view of the great importance these lay ecclesial ministries have assumed in some parts of the Roman Catholic Church. In June 1979 *Pro Vita Mundi*[12] published a dossier on priestless parishes in Western Europe, and attempted solutions. Many parishes are without a priest. According to the *Annuarium Statisticum Ecclesiae – 1976*, over 44,000 parishes are without a resident priest in the Roman Catholic Church but they are looked after by a neighbouring parish priest (and there is naturally scope for lay leadership in such parishes). Apart from those looked after by a male religious, woman religious or permanent deacon, 342 are looked after by lay persons, and 1,474 have no one in charge. With an acute shortage of priests, there is much pastoral care to be undertaken. When visiting the archdiocese of Lyon (the city of Lyon is twinned with the city of Birmingham) I was greatly impressed by the role of the laity not only in preparing people for the baptism of their children, and in taking funerals, etc., but also in distributing holy communion from the reserved sacrament at services over which they presided.

The *Decree on the Apostolate of the Laity* makes provision not merely for the spiritual formation of the laity but also for their solid doctrinal instruction in theology, ethics and philosophy, instruction adapted to differences of age, status and natural talents.[13] Lay people are 'above all to learn the principles and conclusions of the moral and social teaching of the church so as to become capable of doing their part to advance this doctrine and of rightly applying these same principles and conclusions to individual cases.[14] But there is nothing said here about a consideration of the dilemmas of the modern Christian in his daily work, where he is often faced with difficult decisions both with regard to trade union activity or about standards of personal or corporate behaviour; nor is anything said about the difficulty in reaching some moral decisions in matters of great technological complexity where few if any except those actually involved are in a position to know the facts and so bring a moral judgment to bear upon them.

If the role of the laity in the Agreed Statements seems quite compatible with that envisaged in the official documents of the Roman Catholic Church, the same can hardly be said of the Church of England.

In many ways the importance of the lay element was a motivating factor in the Reformation of the English Church. The restoration of the chalice to the laity helped to remove a difference of spiritual status between priests and others. The provision of an open Bible in church, the reading of the Bible in 'the vulgar tongue' and the provision of a liturgy in the vernacular were all oriented towards the laity, judging them capable of making up their own minds if they had open access to the biblical witness. Perhaps most important of all was the assumption by Parliament of powers to order the Church of England, in an age when England was still a Christian land. While the bishops sat in the House of Lords, there was also the Commons of the realm, where lay people could also exercise power over the church. The points have been well put by Professor Stephen Sykes:

Each Christian person in virtue of his or her understanding of the gospel, and readiness to proclaim it, must be held to exercise authority in the Church. The Anglican response to this feature of the New Testament is primarily seen in its insistence that the

Scriptures and the liturgy be heard 'in such a language and order
as is most easy and plain for the understanding both of the readers
and the hearers' (Cranmer, *Concerning the Service of the
Church*). At the time of the Reformation (as now) there might be
heard a great diversity of opinions, both lay and ordained, about
the true doctrine of the Christian religion. To meet this situation
the Anglican reformers provided simple, traditional summaries
of Christian doctrine in the Apostles' and Nicene Creeds, the first
of which was taught in the Catechism, and one or other repeated
at every public service of worship; the open publication and
public reading of the Scriptures ('he that readeth so standing and
turning himself as may be best heard by those present') . . .[15]

In a situation of great perplexity and wide divergence of
theological opinion, it was unquestionably the case that individuals
might well have to decide which of two theological opinions were
correct, and that their lives might even depend on it. Precisely in
such a context, the Anglican reformers opted for the view, deriving
from the New Testament as they understood it, that the gospel
could be apprehended by learned and simple alike, and that it was
part of the responsibility of the minister to equip the whole people
of God with the means for judging aright. It was, and is, the making
of this judgment that gives the laity an invaluable and important
authority in the church of God.

Time has moved forward since the days of the reformers. In 1886
there was set up the first House of Laymen of the Convocation of
Canterbury, with 104 members, and six years later a York House of
Laymen. Shortly after Randall Davidson became Archbishop of
Canterbury in 1903, there was set up the Representative Church
Council consisting of clergy and laity of the Church of England,
formed out of the two Convocations of Canterbury and York and
the two existing Houses of Laymen. By 1913 there was considerable
dissatisfaction at the way in which all church legislation had to go
through the Houses of Parliament, as a result of which there was
eventually set up, after the first Great War (which had intervened)
the Church Assembly, which was able to pass Measures that had
been agreed by all three Houses, of Bishops, of Clergy and of Laity.
These, providing they were agreed by Parliament, became law if
they had the approval of the Ecclesiastical Committee of Parliament, unless either House of Parliament directed by resolution to

the contrary. A measure would not be debated there in detail like a Bill. (There were provisions that made it possible for both Houses to agree a Measure without the agreement of the Ecclesiastical Committee, but that would be an unlikely contingency.) Thus the church assumed a measure of control over its own affairs. In 1920 there were 387 lay members of the Assembly, including 34 women.

The Enabling Act of 1919 not only set up the Church Assembly with these legal powers: it also brought into being Parochial Church Councils (which had among other powers, control over monies given in a church, other than alms at the holy communion) and which had a lay vice-chairman, secretary and treasurer. There was also brought into being the Annual Parochial Church Meeting, which all members of the electoral roll were entitled to attend (and also to ask questions about church affairs); and also the Ruridecanal Conference, and the Diocesan Conference. On all these bodies lay people had their proper place. Thus in the tradition of the Church of England lay people, both men and women, have had an important role and responsibilities to discharge.

In 1948, as a result of a fusion between the Ecclesiastical Commissioners and Queen Anne's Bounty, there was formed the Church Commissioners, with the custodianship of trust funds for the clergy and the care of parsonage houses and churches (in collaboration with dioceses and parishes) as their chief responsibilities. This body is accountable, strictly speaking, to Parliament; but it also renders account of itself to the church. Three lay people are appointed to the executive posts of the three Church Estates Commissioners, and a considerable number of places among the Church Commissioners are reserved for lay people. Accounts are published annually, and even a list of the equities held by the Commissioners. This contrasts with the style of the Roman Catholic Church where parishes do not publish accounts or have church treasurers, but the parish priest takes charge of all monies; and the Vatican Bank (whose funds are undisclosed) is headed by a priest. It is impossible to imagine the kind of scandal which has broken over the head of Archbishop Marcinkus at the Vatican Bank, happening at the Church Commissioners, if only because professional lay people are in charge and accounts are published annually in accordance with charity law.

In 1975 the General Synod was brought into being. Whereas the old Church Assembly could not discuss matters of theology, which were reserved for the two Convocations, the General Synod can and does, and it also passes Canons which previously had been the sole preserve of the Convocations, although provision is still made for meetings of Convocations in certain circumstances. There is an equal number of clergy and laity in General Synod, and (by way of contrast to the Vatican Curia) the influential post of Secretary General is held by a lay person. Similarly, lay people sit on the Crown Appointments Committee (which recommends to the Crown names for nomination to diocesan bishoprics), and on the General Synod's Standing Committee. Whereas those employed in the Roman Catholic curia are Monsignors, posts in Church House are open to clergy and lay people, men and women.

Lay people therefore play a very full part in the life of the Church of England and exercise authority in partnership with bishops and with clergy, although the House of Bishops reserve to themselves certain rights, and some procedures require motions to be passed by a majority (and in some cases a two-thirds majority) of all three Houses.

If in the Church of England the decision-taking body consists of the 'Bishops-in-Synod' (bishops with their representative clergy and laity), the corresponding decision-taking body at a national level in the Roman Catholic Church is the National Episcopal Conference. *In the House of Living God* (a provisional Report from the Bishops' Conference of England and Wales published in 1982) makes it clear that a diocese is the local church in which the universal church of Christ is truly present and active;[16] and yet local churches in a country find it natural to make common cause without becoming a 'national' church. Accordingly episcopal conferences are authorized on a national level together with their various commissions. Earlier these had been so composed as to achieve a balance between experts with technical knowledge and the so-called man-in-the-pew. This system apparently did not work very well. The commissions found it difficult 'to resolve the tension between the consultative and advisory role envisaged for them and their inherent tendency to seek some independence of action'; while 'bishops were known to feel that at times they were swamped by unfamiliar business and in danger of losing control over their agenda and priorities'. A move was put in hand to abandon the inclusion of the 'man-in-the-pew', so that commissions of the Bishops' Conference now consist of only bishops and *periti* (lay persons with special skills). And so, while the Church of England takes its decisions by means of 'Bishops-in-Synod', the Roman Catholic Church in England and Wales takes its decision by a 'Synod of Bishops'; very different indeed.[17]

The structural changes which have given increased authority to lay people have been accompanied by a movement of thought and theology in the same direction, which to a certain extent has been shared by both Roman Catholic and reformed Churches. Charles Davis, before he left the Roman Catholic Church, drew attention[18] to four successive theological cultures in the history of Christendom. Firstly, theology in the patristic age was predominantly episcopal and was a function of pastoral care. The second milieu was monastic, a function of contemplation, motivated by the needs of the ascetic and mystical life, with a strong literary element. (This is still typical of much Eastern theology.) Thirdly, there was scholastic theology, in a university setting, concerned with truth for truth's sake. Mr Davis wrote that, from the Reformation, seminary theology had prevailed, although I do not think that this has really been true of the Church of England, where seminaries are little more than a century old, and in which academic theology has been dominant. This has not always been for the welfare of the Church of England because, for academic and ecumenical reasons, systematic theology has been omitted from university syllabuses, but at least academic theologians have been free from ecclesiastical pressures to conform to the dictates of a hierarchy.

In a recent symposium *All are Called*, authorized by the Church of England's Board of Education, Anthony Dyson emphasizes the importance of the lay contribution:

> If anything, in the process of secularization, clericalism advances its own interests. Clericalism advances the view that as God 'disappears' from secularizing society, so God's presence is concentrated in the institutional, actually defined by patterns of government appropriated from secular society, and by the worship over which the clergy preside.

The lay task, Professor Dyson goes on to say, is found at the creative centre of the culture, 'those critical points of society where God's creativity and redemptive acts are contending with forces of meaninglessness, dispersion, disorder and despair'.[19]

Bishop J. A. T. Robinson, reviewing these eras of theology twenty years ago, called for an era of lay theology, by which he meant a 'worldly divinity' which is not a dilution of academic theology suitable for lay people, but rather a theology which starts from the Christian's involvement in the world now, and which means thinking theologically about this world.[20] More than once he quoted Hans Rudi Weber of the World Council of Churches: 'The laity are not helpers of the clergy so that the clergy can do their job, but the clergy are helpers of the whole people of God, so that the laity can be the Church.' In 1963 Mark Gibbs (who has since devoted his life to lay training) pointed out[21] that new ideas, becoming current in the Church of England, had long been common ground in the German Churches where the Evangelische Akademien and the Kirchentag movements had caught up thousands of lay people; and in the Church of England today many dioceses have instituted 'Foundation Courses' and other types of lay training which lay people have eagerly undertaken.

Mr Oswald Clark, then Chairman of the General Synod's House of Clergy, said in the 1985 General Synod debate on ARCIC: 'The role of the laity is not exhausted by reflection, reception and assent.'[22] Even though Dr Henry Chadwick has explained the reception is not intended to preclude initiative and the exercise of critical judgment,[23] it still does not include the authority to participate in decision-making; and without such authority I would think, so far as Anglicans are concerned, that the ARCIC proposals as they now stand would require modification.

5

The Mother of God Incarnate

The many parish churches the Church of England dedicated to St Mary the Virgin are a testimony to the veneration in which the mother of Jesus was held by those who founded the earliest churches of this land. Since the Reformation of the Church of England, however, her cultus has been minimal, so that many Anglicans today would be surprised (and perhaps even shocked) to discover how highly she was venerated not only in the mediaeval but also in the primitive church.

Mary the mother of Jesus does not figure prominently in the New Testament. Her name is only mentioned nineteen times in its pages, and all but three of those occur during the infancy narratives of St Matthew's and St Luke's Gospels.

Of the three remaining instances, two refer to the incident when Jesus was rejected in his home town of Nazareth, and the last instance refers to her worshipping with the eleven before Pentecost.

There are a few other occasions when reference is made to her without her name being mentioned: when as a teenager Jesus stayed behind in Jerusalem after Passover; at the wedding in Cana of Galilee; at the beginning of Jesus's public ministry when Mary and her family thought that Jesus was out of his mind; when a woman in the crowd cried out about her, and when Jesus 'gave' her to his beloved disciple on the cross.

By the use of Old Testament typology some further understanding about her role may be adduced; that the fruit of her womb is the

Lord God, that she is the 'daughter of Zion' within whom God resides, and that she is the ark of covenant within whom is the very presence of God himself.[1] These all point to her as *theotokos* the Mother of God (or perhaps better, the Mother of God Incarnate) the title that was bestowed upon her officially at the Council of Ephesus (AD 431), and which appears in the Definition of Chalcedon (AD 451), both Councils accepted within the Anglican tradition. From the Gospels we are told that as the mother of Jesus, Mary is to be honoured among all women, that her Son was to be the Son of God and Messiah of Israel, that she became pregnant without human intercourse, and that she willingly accepted her calling.

From these beginnings the cult of Mary developed. Her perpetual virginity was asserted by Hilary of Poitiers in the fourth century, and Didymus gave her the title of 'ever virgin'. Indeed in *The Prot-evangelium of James*, a work of free invention, written after AD 150,[2] Mary is said to be physically a virgin during the miraculous birth of Jesus, a view taught by St Augustine[3] but which never became official doctrine. It was held, however, that the 'brothers' and 'sisters' of Jesus, mentioned in Mark 6.3 and parellels, were really his cousins (a meaning which the Greek could bear).[4] And the title 'ever virgin' was officially bestowed on Mary, and appears in the Vatican II *Dogmatic Constitution on the Church*, which speaks of 'the veneration of the ever virgin Mother of God' (69).

The cult of Mary continued to develop, and in popular piety the representation of the enthroned Virgin with child is similar to that of the typical Isis with her son Horus on her knees. 'This substitution of Mary for the pagan divinities took place partly through a spontane-ous transfer of the popular piety of the converted masses, and, after Constantine, imperfectly converted. In part it corresponded with a programme of exorcising of the pagan cults by the church which destroyed paganism when it could, and when it could not, or found it preferable, took its place by transforming it.'[5] The official cult of Mary, however, is very different from the pagan cults of the mother goddesses. The pagan goddesses are naturalistic in origin and pan-theistic, while the cult of Mary is always connected with the incarn-ation of God in Christ.

Because Mary was hailed as 'full of grace' (Luke 1.28) and because she was *theotokos*, the belief grew that she was all-holy and free from every stain of sin. *The Dogmatic Constitution on the Church* speaks of her thus: 'Mary, daughter of Adam, by consent to the divine word became Jesus' mother, with no sin to hamper her, wholeheartedly embraced God's will of salvation, made a complete dedication of herself as the Lord's handmaid to the person and work of her Son . . .' (56). It was from the conviction that Mary 'had no sin to hamper her' that there later developed the Definition of the Immaculate Conception.

The belief in the sinlessness of Mary, however, is not proved by the scriptures; and indeed there are some pointers against this belief. Paul writes in Rom. 3.23: 'All alike have sinned.' Jesus's somewhat sharp words in John 2.4: 'Woman, what have I to do with thee?' (despite the defences of commentators it was not normal to call one's mother 'Woman') point against her sinlessness: so also does the suggestion in Mark 3.21 that she thought he was out of his mind, and his indifference to her as his mother in Mark 3.33. When the woman in the crowd called out: 'Happy the womb that carried you and the breasts that suckled you' (Luke 11.27), Jesus replied: 'No, happy are those who hear the word of God and keep it' and this seems to imply the possibility of a distinction between his mother and those who keep the word of God. These passages do not prove that Mary was a sinner: what is clear is that no evidence of her sinlessness can be found here.

Devotion to Mary continued to be strong both in the Eastern Church and in the Latin Church during the Middle Ages, and St Thomas Aquinas formulated the doctrine of *hyperdulia* proper to Mary, which, though infinitely inferior to the *latria* (or worship or adoration) due to her Divine Son, yet far surpasses that which is appropriate to angels and saints. This doctrine finds a place in the *Dogmatic Constitution on the Church*: 'She has been raised by God's grace to a position second to her Son above all angels and men' (66). This belief is a matter of faith. It may be held to be consonant with the scriptures but it is not found in them.

There grew up in the church a conviction that Mary, through her function as *theotokos*, had participated actively in the mystery of redemption. Already in the eighth century she had been called Mediatrix by St John of Damascus. By the eighteenth century St Alphonsus of Liguori was maintaining that Mary was Mediatrix of all the graces. These doctrines are not denied in the *Dogmatic Constitution*, nor are they affirmed:

Her motherly love makes her care for her Son's brethren still on their pilgrimage, still involved in dangers and difficulties until they shall be brought to the happiness of their fatherland. For this reason the Blessed Virgin is called upon in the Church under the titles of Advocate, Auxiliatrix, Adjutrix, Mediatrix. Yet this practice is so understood that it represents no derogation from the dignity and efficacy of Christ, the sole Mediator, nor any addition (62).

In the same chapter, the church 'commends to all the faithful, for their heartfelt attention, that they should use the support of his mother's aid to gain a closer adherence to the Mediator and Saviour'.

While undoubtedly this is of help to some, for others it seems to complicate the free access to the Father through Christ which is their birthright as Christians.

Pius IX became Pope in 1846, and it was known that he had a special devotion to the Blessed Virgin Mary, and he received a growing number of requests for the official proclamation of the Doctrine of her Immaculate Conception. After consulting the bishops of the Roman Catholic Church by means of an encyclical, he solemnly proclaimed the doctrine on 8 December 1854:

To the honour of the Holy and Undivided Trinity, to the glory and adornment of the Virgin Mother of God, to the exaltation of the Catholic Faith and the increase of the Christian religion, we, with the authority of our Lord Jesus Christ, the blessed Apostles Peter and Paul, and with our own, do declare, pronounce and define that the doctrine which holds that the Virgin Mary was, in the first instance of her conception, preserved untouched by any taint of original guilt, by a singular grace and privilege of Almighty God, in consideration of the merits of Christ Jesus the Saviour of mankind – that this doctrine was revealed by God and therefore is to be firmly and steadfastly believed by all the faithful. Wherefore if any should presume (which God forbid) to think in their hearts anything contrary to this definition of ours, let them realize and know well that they are condemned by their own judgment, have suffered shipwreck concerning the faith and have revolted from the unity of the Church, and that besides this they do by this subject themselves to the lawful penalties if they shall dare to signify by word or writing or any other external means, what they think in their hearts.

The proclamation of this doctrine was attended by great difficulties.

It could not be demonstrated from the scriptures, and indeed such evidence as I have already adduced may be thought to tend to the contrary. When Jesus was rejected in his home town of Nazareth, the townspeople exclaimed, 'What wisdom is this that has been given him?' and 'How does he work such miracles?' 'Is not this the carpenter, the son of Mary, the brother of James and Joses and Judas and Simon? And are not his sisters with us?' (Mark 6.2ff). The implication of this account is that Mary was an ordinary person, on a par with her sons and daughters (unless of course these be regarded as her nephews and nieces; but in that case the point still holds). Whether Mary was ordinary or not is in a sense beside the point: the scriptures say nothing about her Immaculate Conception, nor could anything be known about it without a special revelation. Certain biblical texts such as 'I shall put enmity between you and the woman, between your blood and hers' (Gen. 3.15) or the Salutation to Mary (Luke 1.28) may or may not be thought consonant with the doctrine, but they in no sense attest it.

Some of the early Fathers (e.g. Justin Martyr) spoke of Mary as the new Eve, and so it was held to follow that Mary, like Eve, was born without the taint of original sin. But this was opposed by notable theologians such as St Bernard, and by most of the schoolmen (e.g. St Bonaventure and St Thomas Aquinas). But Pope Clement XI had imposed the Feast (with its own Mass and Office) on the universal church, and the Council of Trent had excluded the Blessed Virgin Mary from its decree on original sin. The doctrine, although very widespread, cannot be said to have been universally held in Christian tradition.

Nor is it clear what the doctrine means today in the light of modern genetic knowledge. Was Adam's sin a kind of inherited acquired characteristic, which was miraculously excluded from the twenty-three male and twenty-three female chromosomes which Mary inherited from her parents? Some explanations suggest that the miracle of Mary's conception concerned not her physical inheritance, but the infusion of her soul into the embryo or foetus at animation.[6] Such attempted explanations seem to be pre-scientific in their genetic assumptions. There are many explanations of original sin:[7] but it would seem that, if Mary were to be a human being, she would need a normal human inheritance. Indeed St Paul even wrote of Christ that he was 'born in the likeness of sinful flesh'

(Rom. 8.3). Furthermore, if Jesus was to be fully man as well as fully divine (as a true doctrine of the Incarnation requires) he too would need a fully human inheritance; and if the male part were to have been supernaturally supplied, he would still have needed from his mother a normal female inheritance of twenty-three chromosomes. The doctrine of the Immaculate Conception seems hard to reconcile with the requirements of Incarnation or with our modern knowledge of genetics.

The Definition which Pope Pius IX made was proclaimed by him, without the support of an ecumenical council, and it was fraught with the difficulties mentioned above. It is enjoined on Christians in very forthright language, threatening those who do not accept it. Nonetheless, by the time of Vatican II, a century later, enthusiasm for it, or even interest in it, seems to have waned, for in the *Dogmatic Constitution on the Church*, it is mentioned only once *en passant* and in connection with the Doctrine of the Assumption:

> The immaculate Virgin, who had been kept from all stain of original sin, completed the course of her life on earth and was raised, body and soul to the glory of heaven. She has been exalted by the Lord as Queen of all, so as to be more fully modelled on her Son, the Lord of lords, Victor over sin and death (59).

The Doctrine of the Assumption was not defined until 1950 by Pope XII in his Bull *Munificentissimus Deus*, although it has been a popular belief among Christians since long before that. It seems that the idea of a bodily assumption first arose in gnostic heterodox circles. It is hardly convincing to suggest, as some have done, that a tradition of silence about this matter was deliberately maintained in the church, so that there would be no confusion in the early church between Mary and her Son; nor is it satisfactory to assert that a continuous oral tradition of the Assumption was in fact maintained from New Testament times, but it received so little emphasis that it does not appear in any of the documents which have come down to us. The first mention of the corporal Assumption of Mary appears in a gnostic apocryphal work *The Passing of Mary* which has come down to us in many translations. The Greek text appears to be oldest, and apparently cannot be assigned to a date later than the fourth century.[8] Some confusion is caused because the word *assumptio*, which literally means God's taking to himself the Blessed Virgin (e.g. by death), is used in ancient writers and in ancient liturgies with that meaning rather than to imply the Virgin's corporal assumption. The story of the corporal Assumption first appears in orthodox circles in the writings of the sixth century Gregory of Tours.[9] The Assumption became associated with the belief that the event took place in the tomb ascribed to her in the Garden of Gethsemane, and the belief gained credence by the inclusion in the Breviary in the sixteenth century of an account by the eighth-century St John Damascene of her assumption from this tomb in the presence of the apostles.

If the historical evidence for the doctrine seems slight, what can be said about the theological arguments?

So far as the scriptures are concerned, texts are adduced which may be said to fall into three classes; texts which show Mary's pre-eminence (e.g. Luke 1.28), texts which in a figurative sense could be understood to refer to the Assumption (e.g. Psalm 44.9, 'Upon thy right hand stood the Queen in gold of Ophir'.) and texts from the Book of Revelation, chapter 12, which are obscure in meaning. The doctrine cannot be established by scriptural arguments, and if the Immaculate Conception is not consonant with them, neither is the Assumption. It is said that it follows on from that of the Immaculate Conception. If Mary did not sin, it has been suggested that it was inappropriate for her to die, or least to remain dead, and so her body was taken with her soul to heaven. Again, if Mary's flesh gave rise to that of the Incarnate Lord, her flesh could be said to be consubstantial with his, and if his divine flesh was assumed into heaven, it is fitting that the same thing befell his mother's. If her flesh was incorruptible, it was not fitting that it should remain on earth.

These arguments are likely to carry weight in accordance with a predisposition to believe the doctrine. In fact the doctrine was proclaimed by Pope Pius XII because so many already did believe it. A request had been made way back in 1849 that the Assumption should be defined along with the Immaculate Conception. This request was not granted. Then came Vatican I and the definition of Papal Infallibility. The use of this power seemed to have been kept in abeyance, but popular devotion to Mary suggested its use. Between 1863 (when Isabella II of Spain began this popular movement) and 1920 over 3,000 petitions for the definition, containing over 8,000,000 signatures, reached Rome. On 8 December 1950, during the Marian Year, Pope Pius XII issued an Apostolic Constitution:

By the authority of our Lord Jesus Christ, and of the Blessed
Apostles Peter and Paul and of our own, we pronounce, declare
and define it to be a divinely revealed dogma that Mary, the
Immaculate Ever Virgin Mother of God, when the course of her
earthly life was run, was assumed to heavenly glory in body and
soul.

It may be noted that this did not appear to the faithful of the time
to add to the deposit of faith, since it was already such a
widespread belief among Roman Catholics (so much so that when
the Pope consulted bishops before defining the doctrine, those
opposed to the Definition did not, and perhaps could not, say it
was untrue, but only that it was inopportune). It may also be noted
that definitions of the faith are intended to be used in order to
resolve difficulties and to apply papal authority to situations where
there is confusion. But in this case there seemed to be no confusion, and the definition seemed to be made so as to give honour to
Mary rather than to resolve controversy about her. Like the earlier
Marian doctrine, this Definition was made by the Pope, independently exercising his power of Infallibility which was defined at
Vatican I as inhering in his office, and he did not summon a
Council to make the Definition with him.

It has already been remarked that the *Dogmatic Constitution on
the Church* of Vatican II makes only one mention of the Assumption, when it describes Mary as Queen of all (59). This description
of Mary follows naturally from her exalted position as having
the pre-eminence over all created beings in heaven. It also explains the frequent invocation of her prayers by faithful Roman
Catholics.

The language of the *Dogmatic Constitution on the Church* is very
cautious and restrained compared with earlier official statements
about Mary. Indeed 'This Synod earnestly exhorts theologians and
preachers of the divine word that in treating of the unique dignity of
the Mother of God, they carefully and equally avoid the falsity of
exaggeration on the one hand, and the excess of narrow-minded-
ness on the other . . . Let them painstakingly guard against any
word or deed which could lead separated brethren or anyone else
into error regarding the true doctrine of the Church' (67). (The
same caution is to be found in Pope Paul VI's Apostolic Exhortation
Marialis Cultus (24).)

Since Anglicans fall within the category of separated brethren, the question must be asked: what is the official doctrine of the Church of England about Mary?

In the first place, it must be noted that due liturgical honour is given to her in the liturgy by naming feast days in her honour. The Book of Common Prayer contains the Feast of the Purification of Mary the Blessed Virgin, the Annunciation of the Blessed Virgin Mary, the Visitation of the Blessed Virgin Mary, and even commemorates her Conception on 8 December. In the liturgy the Creeds, with their affirmation of the Virginal Conception, are frequently recited, and this is again emphasized in the Proper Preface for Christmas Day. Apart from the affirmation of the Incarnation in Article II ('took Man's nature in the womb of the blessed Virgin, of her substance'), Mary is not mentioned in the Articles of Religion. The phrase 'Mother of God' is unknown to Anglican liturgy. As for the doctrines of the perpetual virginity of Mary, her Immaculate Conception and her Assumption, no mention is made of them in official Anglican documents; and in so far as they are not read in scripture, and cannot be proved thereby, they cannot be said to be requisite or necessary to salvation (Article VI). Mary is given great honour, respect and affection as the one person chosen by God to bear in her womb his Son; but she is not given *hyperdulia*, the special veneration over and above that given to saints and angels. Such phrases as Mediatrix, Auxiliatrix, Adjutrix and Advocate are foreign to Anglicanism. Although some churches honour the 'dormition' (or falling asleep) of Mary, the doctrine of her bodily assumption into heaven is not an Anglican dogma, although a member of the Church of England is free to hold any of these Marian doctrines as a matter of personal faith. They do not form part of the public faith of the church. They seem to most Anglicans to be well grounded neither in scripture nor in the primitive tradition of the church (so far as the Roman Catholic officially defined Marian dogmas are concerned) and they do not seem to confirm to the Anglican canon of sound learning. Furthermore Anglicans do not believe that the Bishop of Rome has power to define doctrine on his own (without the consent of an ecumenical council) and so they are unable to accept these doctrines by the authority of the Pope alone.

Furthermore there are members of the Church of England who are agnostic about the Virginal Conception of Jesus and some who believe that, while it is to be valued for the truths that it expresses, it

does not contain historical truth. Although the formularies of the
Church of England clearly state belief in the Virginal Conception, it
is in accordance with the ethos of the church to allow its members a
liberty of belief in this matter. A statement on this subject in
Doctrine in the Church of England (1938) runs as follows:

> . . . Many of us accordingly hold that belief in the Word made
> flesh is integrally bound up with belief in the Virgin Birth, and
> that this will increasingly be recognized.
>
> There are, however, some among us who hold that a full belief
> in the historical Incarnation is more consistent with the supposi-
> tion that our Lord's birth took place under the normal conditions
> of human generation. In their minds, the notion of a Virgin Birth
> tends to mar the completeness of the belief that in the Incarnation
> God revealed Himself at every point in and through human
> nature.
>
> We are agreed in recognizing that belief in our Lord's birth
> from a Virgin has been in the history of the Church intimately
> bound and associated with its faith in the Incarnation of the Son
> of God. Further, we recognize that the work of scholars upon the
> New Testament has created a new setting of which theologians in
> their treatment of this article are bound to take account. We also
> recognize that both the views outlined above are held by
> members of the Church, as of the Commission, who fully accept
> the reality of our Lord's Incarnation, which is the central truth of
> the Christian faith.[10]

Does such a belief lower Mary in the moral estimation of
Christians? It must be remembered that, if Joseph were the natural
father of Jesus, sexual relations in Galilee commonly commenced at
betrothal. Furthermore, the surprising inclusion of three women in
the Matthean genealogy (Rahab, Ruth and Tamar), two of whom
are connected with some sexual irregularity, seems to be intended
to show that the divine purpose of redemption has worked through
human weakness. In John 6.42 the Jews say: 'Is not this Jesus the
son of Joseph, from whom was begotten Jesus who was called the
Christ?', while the Jews retort in John 8.21, 'We are not born from
fornication.' The description of Jesus by the Jews in Mark 6.3 as
'son of Mary' makes use of a form of words used of one born out of
wedlock. The Matthaean genealogy suggests Joseph as father.

Another explanation has been put forward by Professor Reuther, a Roman Catholic scholar. She has suggested that in the earliest Christian traditions the idea that God specially intervened in Jesus' birth does not exclude the fatherhood of Joseph.

The young Mary might have been thought of as a girl who is betrothed at too early an age to be fertile (a not uncommon practice at this time) and who conceives before menstruation gives the first evidence of her fertility. Rabbinic writings refer to such births as 'virgin births'. So God's miraculous intervention does not need to exclude Joseph's biological role.[11]

None of these considerations in any way disproves the historical account of the Virginal Conception of Jesus, nor need they have any bearing on the eternal truths which this story expresses (that Jesus is the Son of God, and that God made a fresh start for humanity in Jesus). They do, however, help to explain the 'new setting' of which scholars must take account, and it affords a good illustration of the liberty of interpretation which the Church of England commonly affords her members.

When we turn from the doctrine of the Roman Catholic Church and of the Church of England about the Blessed Virgin Mary and examine the ARCIC Agreed Statements on the doctrines concerning her, we find that comment has been compressed into a single paragraph.[12]

Paragraph 30 of Authority in the Church II begins by remarking that the Marian definitions are the only examples of such dogmas promulgated by the Bishop of Rome apart from a synod since the separation of our two communions, a point already noted earlier in this chapter. The Statement then continues: 'Anglicans and Roman Catholics can agree in much of the truth that these two dogmas are designed to affirm.'

The Statement goes on to illustrate this by some examples. 'We agree that there can be but one mediator between God and man, Jesus Christ, and reject any interpretation of the role of Mary which obscures this affirmation.' This sentiment happily concurs with a similar Statement in the *Dogmatic Constitution on the Church* (62), but it is hardly directly relevant to the Definitions on the Immaculate Conception and the Assumption to which reference has been made. The Statement continues: 'We agree in recognizing that Christian understanding of Mary is inseparably linked with the doctrines of Christ and of the Church.' This is somewhat broader than the *Dogmatic Constitution on the Church* where it is said that the 'functions and privileges of the Blessed Virgin' are 'always relative to Christ, the origin of truth, holiness and piety' (67, with no mention of the church).

The Statement continues in expressing agreement on the grace given to and the unique vocation of Mary and that 'she was prepared by divine grace to be the mother of our Redeemer, by whom she herself was redeemed and received into glory'. This is certainly common ground.

The next point, however, might not be so universally agreed by Anglicans. 'We further agree in recognizing in Mary a model of holiness, obedience and faith for all Christians.' Certainly perfect obedience and faith are shown in the story of the Annunciation, and here lies a model for all Christians; but this one instance does not make Mary's life *as a whole* necessarily a model for all Christians, especially in the light of the interpretations of some sayings in the Gospels which I have suggested may show her in a light which falls short of perfection.

The Agreed Statement next refers to the problems that the two Definitions cause for Anglicans because they may not consider that they are sufficiently supported by the scriptures, and because they rest on the teaching authority of the Bishop of Rome independent of a council. Anglicans, it is said, would ask whether they would be required to subscribe to such dogmatic statements. It is not easy to see how a doctrine which at the time of its Definition was thought to be so important that those who did not believe it had 'made shipwreck of their faith' could now be thought to be sufficiently expendable that ex-Anglicans in any scheme of organic reunion would not be required to subscribe to it. To permit this might seem likely to overthrow the authority attaching to the Bishop of Rome that is characteristic of the Roman Catholic Church. Nor would it be satisfactory for Anglicans to say that they believed in the truths to which these dogmas point without believing in the historical components of the dogmas themselves. For that would open the way towards saying that belief in the physical resurrection was unimportant providing that the spiritual truths of the resurrection were believed. It would assault the sacramental principle whereby God expresses himself by outward means in order to signify and effect a spiritual truth.

Paragraph 30 in the Agreed Statement concludes with these words:

> One consequence of our separation has been a tendency for Anglicans and Roman Catholics alike to exaggerate the importance of the Marian dogmas in themselves at the expense of other truths more closely related to the foundation of the Christian faith.

As a statement of fact that is no doubt true. The effect of theological controversy is often to concentrate on matters of secondary importance. On the other hand it does not affect the *truth* of a statement to say that it takes a low place in the hierarchy of truth. Once a statement has been (infallibly) defined as true, it is very difficult to say that it is unimportant, although it is quite possible to consider that it was at the time given exaggerated importance. Perhaps Marian dogmas could be stated today in different terms, although no one has attempted this. It is sometimes thought that these Marian dogmas – showing the functions, honour and privileges given to a purely human figure – were needed at a time when Jesus himself was regarded as not fully human but rather one whose divinity was thinly veiled by flesh. If Jesus were considered primarily as divine Judge, then a human person overflowing with compassion would make a natural balance, especially if the compassionate figure were female, contrasting with the rest of the cultus and a theology which were both largely male-dominated. Today the cultural and theological background has changed; and in these altered circumstances, the Marian dogmas may be of less psychological importance. But that is not the real point at issue. The real questions concern whether these truths are literally true, whether they are fully supported by the scriptures, whether the Bishop of Rome can define them independently of scripture. However low they may figure in the hierarchy of truth, it would hardly be possible to frame a scheme of organic reunion between Anglicans and Roman Catholics on the proviso either that Anglicans would have to subscribe to them, or that they become optional for Roman Catholics.

6

Traditions of Ethical Thinking

Catholics and Protestants have tended in the past to develop different traditions in their thinking about personal and social behaviour. Catholics have developed complex systems of moral theology, while Protestants have tended to think in terms of what they have called 'Christian ethics'.

Catholics have accepted from Greek thought the four cardinal virtues of justice, prudence, temperance and courage; and they have added to these the three theological virtues of faith, hope and love. From these they have tended to build up on the basis of the scriptural revelation what are called 'middle axioms' of Christian behaviour, that is to say, general statements of what is right. They have evolved various principles by which to apply these 'middle axioms' to particular cases. Probabilism is a system which regards it right to act on the basis that a particular action is probably right, while probabiliorism justifies an act on the grounds that it is more probably right than any other possibility. Tutiorism, the most acceptable system, justifies an action on the ground that it is 'safer' than other possible actions. This introduction to casuistry shows something of the complexity of moral judgments. Casuistry earned itself a bad reputation under Jesuit influence during the Counter Reformation, but it is essential in a system of moral reasoning of this kind, because otherwise the church could give no assistance to individuals in their actual moral dilemmas.

Protestants, however, have approached these problems from

quite a different point of view. As they see things, man always stands before God as a sinner, and all his apparent worth and goodness is as filthy rags. And so Protestants have tended to fight shy of any system of ethics which seems to attribute worth to the actions of sinful humanity. Out of his sovereign grace God may choose to forgive us; but that does not mean that we have thereby become righteous. We have, however, been placed in a right relationship with God, and thereby enabled to be in a right relationship with other people. It is only when man is reconciled to God that his conscience no longer accuses him, and God's grace enables him to act rightly. Then, as he follows in the way of Christ with a good conscience and under the impulse of the Holy Spirit, he can do works pleasing to God. Christian ethics is concerned with man under grace enabled to keep the commandments of God and to apply them to his life. Just as Protestants tend to ignore or deny natural theology, so also they tend to ignore or deny natural law, and concentrate on scripture.

The Church of England, which claims to be both catholic and reformed, has no one particular rationale of Christian behaviour. It has not officially endorsed any system of moral theology; nor has it developed its own thinking about Christian ethics. Unlike the Roman Catholic Church, it does not have a clearcut authoritative teaching on Christian conduct; but on the other hand it does not leave its members without any guidance on these matters, such as some Protestant Churches do, as though they were entirely matters for private judgment. That is not to say, of course, that there are not particular moral theologians within Anglicanism who have adopted Catholic or Protestant norms of ethical thinking. Dr R. C. Mortimer, for example, developed an Anglican moral theology akin to the Roman Catholic model in his *Elements of Moral Theology*;[1] while Canon Douglas Rhymes developed a form of situational ethics based on the sole principle of love in his *No-New Morality*.[2] In point of fact moral theology has been much neglected in the Church of England. It flourished briefly in the seventeenth century under such thinkers as Jeremy Taylor, and Kenneth Kirk initiated a revival of interest during this century. The church itself, before the setting up of the Board for Social Responsibility under the Church Assembly and later under General Synod, had no means of expressing its corporate viewpoint, apart from matters under review at Lambeth Conferences, which only took place at ten year intervals.

How are moral judgments to be made? It would seem that three considerations are always needed if a proper judgment is to be effected. These considerations are 1. a moral consideration of the nature of the act, 2. a consideration of the probable consequences arising from the action and 3. the intention of the agent in carrying out an action. Many people in fact judge the morality of an action simply by its consequences, whether intended or not. Such bare 'utilitarianism' (which may be much more sophisticated in its formulation than a consideration of mere consequences) is unacceptable to Christian conscience, because it is concerned solely with ends and not with means. The Protestant approach has tended to be concerned only with a person's inner attitudes, based usually on those precepts of Jesus which concentrate on a 'pure intention'; and Protestantism has tended to assume that only those whose spiritual lives have been renewed in Christ are capable of a 'pure intention'. Catholicism on the other hand has concentrated – or seems to have concentrated – on the natural law, and so it has given prime consideration to the nature of the act. The discipline of auricular confession, after which advice is given by the confessor to the penitent, has created a need for a system which gives detailed guidance and which its clergy would be likely to operate; and a certain legalism which has always been characteristic of the Western Church (in contrast to the Eastern Church) from earliest days has tended to encourage this tendency towards authoritative codes of behaviour. (Nonetheless the 'internal forum of conscience' has not been neglected, and it is recognized that a person has a duty not only to inform his conscience but also to act in accordance with it, even though objectively it may be held to be in error.) This legalistic tendency has resulted in great importance being attached to Canon Law, in contrast to the Church of England where the revision of pre-Reformation Canon Law was only completed a quarter of a century ago!

Furthermore, the magisterium of the Roman Catholic Church claims jurisdiction over questions of morals as much as over matters of faith:

Let no Catholic be heard to assert that the interpretation of the natural moral law is outside the competence of the Church's Magisterium. It is in fact indisputable, our Predecessors have many times declared, that Jesus Christ, when he communicated his divine power to Peter and the other apostles and sent them to teach all men his commandments, constituted them as the authentic guardians and interpreters of the whole moral law, not only that of the law of the gospel, but also of the natural law, the reason being that the natural law declares the will of God, and its faithful observance is necessary to man's eternal salvation.[3]

Anglicans of course would not agree that it is 'indisputable' that the Roman Catholic magisterium has power to interpret all natural moral laws. However, those same Anglicans would not find it easy to explain the principles on which they are given guidance on moral matters!

There is not much to be found in those three primary sources of authority for the Church of England; the Thirty-nine Articles of Religion, the Book of Common Prayer and the Ordinal.

So far as the Thirty-nine Articles are concerned, only three of them concern matters of morality (although the commendation found in them of the Second Book of Homilies show that there were plenty of other moral matters to be preached about). The three Articles in question all deal with matters controversial at the time when the Articles were written; Article XXXVII deals with pacificism, Article XXXVIII with community of goods, Article XXXIX with swearing on oath. They give moral judgments with the minimum of reasoning.

As for the Book of Common Prayer, one of the rubrics to the service of Holy Communion provides for the possibility of excommunication in the case of an open and notorious evil liver or someone who has wronged his neighbour in such a way that the congregation has been offended; but the wrongdoing is in no way defined. As for any 'betwixt whom he perceives malice and hatred to reign', a clergyman should excommunicate them until such time as they be reconciled. The repetition of the Ten Commandments at every celebration of the Holy Communion according to the Book of Common Prayer shows the importance attached to right conduct; but no guidance is given about how to apply the Ten Commandments to the actual situations of everyday life. This was left to the private judgment of the individual, aided by pastoral advice from the priest.

One of the sections of the Catechism in the Book of Common Prayer is concerned with moral teaching. First, the catechist requires a person to recite the Ten Commandments, and then he is asked

'What dost thou chiefly learn by these Commandments?' When answers are given to the question 'What is thy duty towards thy neighbour?', the commandments are expanded somewhat. Among others, I am to 'love, honour and succour my father and mother', a commandment which obviously predates social security benefits and pensions. I am to 'submit myself to all my governors, teachers, spiritual pastors and masters', which suggests a disciplinarian approach not always thought desirable today. I am to 'order myself lowly and reverently to all my betters', a command which presupposes a more hierarchical order of society than obtains today. I am to 'keep my hands from picking and stealing', a commandment which is alas all too little honoured but which by its wording suggests a law for the poor rather than for the rich. I am not 'to covet nor desire other men's goods; but to learn and labour truly to get mine own living', an admirable exhortation to self-help, but one which presupposes an order of society where no one need be unemployed. Furthermore, I am 'to do my duty in that state of life, unto which it shall please God to call me'. This suggests that it is wrong to attempt to rise from one social class to another, unless God clearly calls a person to do so. The other clauses of the Catechism not mentioned here are more general and therefore uncontroversial, but those commented on above show the need to bring moral teaching up to date in accordance with the circumstances in which they are to be applied. That is partly the reason that the Church of England has issued a Revised Catechism.

Canon Law adds little more here to these sources of Anglican authority. Canon B 6 I requires Sunday to be marked by 'abstention from all unnecessary labour and business'. Holy Matrimony is defined as 'in its nature permanent and lifelong' (Canon C 10 3 b). According to Canon C 4 3, no one can be ordained who has remarried during the lifetime of a former spouse (or who is married to a spouse who has remarried and whose former husband is living), and a priest may be refused institution to a benefice on the grounds of 'pecuniary embarrassment of a serious character, misconduct or neglect of duty in an ecclesiastical office, evil life, having by his conduct caused grave scandal concerning his moral character since his ordination' (Canon D 10 3 b); but these impediments are not further defined. Canon Law is only binding on the clergy, but of course their actions can have great effects on the lives of lay people, as for instance in the matter of remarriage in church. In fact remarriage in church is not forbidden by Canon Law, because, being part of the law of the realm, it must not conflict with statute law, which has the pre-eminence. Nonetheless, the rulings of the Convocations of the Church have forbidden clergy to solemnize remarriages in church, which officially gives the Church of England the strictest marriage discipline in Christendom. (Roman Catholics have a 'safety valve' in nullity, the Orthodox and Protestant Churches may permit re-marriage in church.)

When we compare Roman Catholic official teaching on morals with Anglican teaching, we are hardly comparing like with like, because (apart from the Catechism) most Anglican teaching belongs to this century, while Roman Catholics have a long history of Bulls and encyclicals running back through the centuries. Of course not all Roman Catholic teaching is of the same authority. None of it has been stamped with infallibility. However, where there has been a constant Roman Catholic tradition of moral thinking, this has been understood as the guidance of the Holy Spirit and it is very difficult for it to be changed. An examination of the encyclical *Humanae Vitae* shows how conscious Pope Paul VI was of the constant tradition of the church against artificial contraception; and to break that tradition would undermine the very authority of the church on which all subsequent pronounce-ments would rest.

Can the Roman Catholic Church change its mind on moral matters? It certainly has done in the matter of usury. As late as 1745 the then Pope insisted that interest on all loans for consumption should be repaid, and a hundred years later Rome tried (unsuccess-fully) to apply this universally. However, the civil law began to change. Interest on loans at 5% became legal in Germany in the sixteenth century, and interest in France was allowed in 1789. The Roman Catholic Church never formulated a decree to make interest lawful, but in the 1830s replies from the Holy Office admitted its lawfulness.[4]

Thus the Roman Catholic Church has changed its mind on an important matter of morals which lies at the heart of the capitalist system. It ought to be said, however, that the reason for the veto on interest (derived from the Old Testament) was the protection of the borrower; but, as circumstances changed, money was no longer borrowed in order to meet the borrower's immediate needs, but in order to create wealth. The borrower could be protected without an absolute ban on all interest, a ban which anyway it was possible to bypass in most cases. The circumstances in which the moral teaching was to be applied had largely changed; and in those circumstances the Roman Catholic teaching also changed. However, so far as the Church of England is concerned, the possibility of change arises not only when circumstances change, but also when new light is shed on the nature of the act (as in contraception, and also, as we shall see in the next chapter, on matters concerning human fertilization). A reformed church can admit the possibility of error.

Perhaps the greatest difference between the two communions lie in the authority to be attached to the official teaching of the church. Although in fact lay members of the Church of Rome (and even clergy) may at times sit light to the official teaching of that church, the magisterium claims to give authoritative teaching to the whole church. There is no question of the moral teaching being tested by reception. For example, it is well known that the encyclical *Humanae Vitae* is to a great extent ignored by lay members of the church. There was a time when those who used artificial methods of contraception were denied the sacraments, as being in 'mortal sin'. However, nowadays this is no longer the case, and many Roman Catholics do not think it necessary to mention their use at auricular confession, if indeed they make use of that sacrament. But, officially at least, it has not been suggested that the fact that this encyclical has not been generally received in any way casts doubt upon its authoritativeness. By contrast, it is not generally thought in the Church of England that the fact that the General Synod has pronounced on some moral topic makes such a judgment in any way authoritatively binding on the conscience of all members of that church, although if there was a sufficient consensus, such a pronouncement would be regarded as having more authority. Likewise a pronouncement by the House of Bishops on some moral topic (if it were to happen that they were to issue such a pronouncement independently of the other two Houses) would also be regarded as having some authority. Anglican ethical pronouncements provide guidance rather than authoritative rulings. In the same way, the Resolutions of Lambeth Conference are not binding upon the constituent churches of the Anglican Communion, but they do provide authoritative guidance to those churches.

These generalizations may be illustrated by a consideration of moral teaching in particular fields.

It is during the present century that the Roman Catholic Church has developed its social teaching by a series of remarkable encyclicals. In 1961 Pope John XXIII issued *Mater et Magistra*. This encyclical shows the importance, already noted, of bringing up to date the thinking of the church, for it contains a re-evaluation of social questions after the publication of *Rerum Novarum* by Pope Leo XIII in 1891, and *Quadragesimo Anno* by Pope Pius XI forty years later. The right to private property is affirmed in all three encyclicals, but Pope John XXIII has a much warmer appreciation of socialization. His encyclical letter contains comments on a very broad front, and goes into considerable detail, especially on new aspects of social problems, and on the rebuilding of a new social order based on truth, justice and love. Theology, however, is surprisingly low key throughout this letter.

Pope John XXIII issued in 1963 a further encyclical letter, *Pacem in Terris*, which deals with social questions in a more fundamental way. It is concerned with human rights and duties, relations between individuals and the public authorities within a single state, relations between states and the relationship of men and of political communities with the world community. The social thinking of the church from *Rerum Novarum* down to the encyclicals of John XXIII were summarized in a document of the Second Vatican Council of exceptional length, *Gaudium et Spes*, which ranges over the whole field of human life, and which includes sections on the family, the proper development of culture, principles governing socio-economic life, the life of the political community, the fostering of peace and the promotion of a community of nations. These systematic studies on social ethics are of the greatest value and importance, whether or not there is general agreement on their contents; and the Anglican Church has nothing comparable, other than particular studies of particular problems of social concern (e.g. the publications of the Board for Social Responsibility and the resulting debates and resolutions of the General Synod), or the reports and resolutions of successive Lambeth Conferences.

Pope Paul VI in 1967 issued *Populorum Progressio*, which was a theological study and appraisal of developmental issues in the Third World. In 1981 Pope John Paul II issued *Laborem Exercens*, on the ninetieth anniversary of *Rerum Novarum*, a theological and social

study on the theme of work, dealing with work and man, the conflict
between labour and capital in the present phase of history, the rights
of workers, and elements for a spirituality of work. In the same year
there was also published the Apostolic Exhortation of Pope John
Paul II called *Familiaris Consortio*, following a Synod of bishops,
concerning the role of the Christian family in the modern world. Both
of these enlarged on the material found in the earlier encyclicals.

The Church of England has nothing to correspond to these systematic expositions of Christian social thinking. This does not mean,
however, that there has not grown up a corpus of Anglican social
theology and ethical thinking. What has happened is that various
issues have been considered piecemeal with reference to actual
situations; and the fundamental theological and ethical principles
have been expounded with reference to these actual real-life
situations. These are not always (but generally) in accord with the
principles expounded in the Roman Catholic encyclical letters; and
in each case a report has been issued rather than authoritative
expositions and definitions. These reports have been in most cases
considered by the General Synod and in many cases sent down to
diocesan synods (and at their discretion to deanery synods) for
discussion and comment. Some are purely educational documents,
such as *Prison and Prisoners in England Today* (1978), *Housing and
Homelessness* (1982), *Perspectives in Economics* (1984).[5] Generally
the Board's documents attempt to spread understanding and at times
questioning. Whereas the Roman Catholic Church tends to produce
authoritative statements to be received from the magisterium by the
rest of the church (suggesting the old distinction between *ecclesia
discens* and *ecclesia docens*), the Church of England has tended to
produce documents on controversial matters about which it expects
discussion and appraisal in the hope of gaining a consensus viewpoint
in the church; but it has always accepted the fact that (as in the case
of remarriage in church or attitudes towards homosexuality) there
may be continuing conflict before that consensus can be achieved.
Occasionally essays have been produced giving two sides of a question without any attempt at reconciling them, as in *Transnational
Corporations* (1983) and *Growth, Justice and Work* (1985).

An example of some divergence between Roman Catholic social
thinking and that of the Church of England could be the question of
human rights. Pope John XXIII in *Pacem in Terris* developed at some
length the concept of human rights from the idea of man's dignity as

made in God's image.[6] The Church of England, through its Board for Social Responsibility, noted that the concept originally derived from Greek philosophy, and then took shape as 'human rights' against 'the power of the state', and took expression in the American Declaration of Independence, and was later developed in this century in e.g. the UN Universal Declaration of Human Rights, and the 1976 Recommendations on Human Rights by the World Council of Churches.[7] At the same time the Board for Social Responsibility document drew some distinctions which differed both from these and from those outlined in *Pacem in Terris*:

> Inherent or inalienable rights can be established on the basis of the doctrine of the image of God when we consider those human characteristics which are both distinctively human and shared with God, e.g. intellectual, moral and spiritual consciousness, and a capacity for personal relationships. Any action which diminishes or destroys those faculties is to be deplored, since it infringes man's inherent right to be what he is – a being made in God's image. Thus the use of torture, brain operations, drugs which make a man mad; brainwashing techniques for eliminating his moral consciousness, prolonged solitary confinement and whatever eliminates a man's capacities for personal relationships – all these may be regarded as interfering with inherent human rights.[8]

This analysis in no way denies the six human rights enumerated in the Fifth Assembly of the World Council of Churches, or the human rights expounded in *Pacem in Terris*, but it argues in greater depth and with more sophistication about this subject of such deep concern to the human race.

An interesting contrast to the environmental ethics of *Populorium Progressio* is the emphasis on trade not aid in the Anglican *Let Justice Flow* (1986). A significant contrast between the methodology of the two churches is afforded by the subject of work. Pope John Paul II's encyclical letter *Laborem Exercens* is a systematic and authoritative study of the theme of work, building on previous encyclicals and developing its thesis from biblical foundations. By contrast, the Church of England's Board for Social Responsibility produced a much briefer report (which was endorsed by its General Synod) entitled *Work and the Future* (1979) which was particularly oriented towards an emergent situation, but which nonetheless built upon biblical foundations. It was subtitled 'technology, world development and jobs in the eighties'. This work was studied at local levels in several dioceses of the church.

One aspect of social ethics in which the Church of England have taken an interest which seems to be lacking in the great Roman Catholic documents on social ethics is the human environment. The Church of England issued a report in the days when this was as yet a comparatively unknown subject. *Man in his Living Environment* was published in 1970, and a return to the subject has recently been made in the Report *Our Responsibility for the Living Environment* (1986). The concern has been developed from the theological base of God's creation of the world and of man's stewardship within it.

Questions of human rights have been applied in the church to racial minorities and (as in the case of South Africa) to racial majorities who have been subject to restrictions. *Facing the Facts* (1982) explains the reasons why Great Britain has a special responsibility towards the situation of apartheid as it has developed in South Africa, and it is perhaps written not so much theologically as in terms of political change. The subject of racism is, however, treated more fundamentally in a series of occasional papers issued from time to time under the title *Theology and Racism*, the first number of which dealt with antisemitism, and the second with racism in the churches today.

Two further major subjects in social ethics have been tackled by the Board for Social Responsibility of the Church of England. One concerns dying, and the other concerns nuclear defence.

Way back in 1959 the Board issued a report *Ought Suicide to be a Crime?* While this, as so much social thinking in the Church of England, was oriented towards a change in the secular law, it approached the subject theologically, and concluded that the state should show its concern by means which lie outside the penal code. Much later, in 1975, the Board issued a report *On Dying Well*, which was an Anglican contribution to the debate on euthanasia. (This was a secular rather than a theological debate, and evoked the response *Death with Dignity* [1976] from the Voluntary Euthanasia Society.) The Anglican report concluded that it can be quite legitimate to enable a patient to die with dignity without attempting to preserve life by artificial means, and that drugs should be given for the relief of pain even where there is a risk that they may shorten life, but that a change in the law which permits euthanasia would not remove greater evils than it would cause.[9] This is similar to the conclusions of the Congregation of the Faith's *Declaration on Euthanasia* (1980).

While mankind, especially in the West, has been living under the shadow of the nuclear threat, it is appropriate to ask what contributions the churches have made to thinking on this subject. The Second Vatican Council document *Gaudium et Spes* has important sections on peace making, total war, and curbing the savagery of war (77–82). Pope John Paul II, in a 'Message to UN Special Session on Disarmament' on 11 June 1982 said:

> In current conditions 'deterrence' based on balance, certainly not as an end in itself but as a step on the way towards progressive disarmament, may still be judged morally acceptable. Nevertheless, in order to ensure peace, it is indispensable not to be satisfied with this minimum which is always susceptible to the real danger of explosion.

While the Roman Catholic Church has issued authoritative statements on nuclear defence from Rome, episcopal conferences have developed fuller statements after a process of considerable consultation, not only with Rome, but with all shades of opinion. Thus the United States Roman Catholic Bishops issued a Pastoral Letter on war and peace in the nuclear age entitled *The Challenge of Peace: God's Promise and our Response* (1983),[10] which earned widespread respect.

The Church of England has only arrived at a viewpoint on these matters after long and open debate, but even so its official attitude does not represent the views of all its members, many of whom are members of organizations which favour unilateral disarmament. Way back in 1973 the Board published *Force in the Modern World* which brought together studies on a number of matters concerning security, violence, non-violence and the peaceful use of military forces. These were discussion documents rather than authoritative statements. In 1979 the General Synod urged the Board to continue its studies on how the theological debate on matters concerning the promotion and preservation of peace could best be conducted. The Board, which had already produced a report on *Christians in a Violent World*,[11] set up a new Working Party which produced in 1982 its report *The Church and the Bomb*,[12] which was a fundamental discussion of nuclear deterrence and which among many uncontroversial recommendations, proposed that the United Kingdom should renounce its independent nuclear deterrent, cancel Trident, and phase out nuclear weapons wholly or mainly of British manufacture, US nuclear weapons, US base facilities, and (the then) projected Cruise missiles. These proposals led to a lively debate both in the church and in the country as a whole, and at a widely publicised all-day debate the General Synod in February 1983 drastically revised them:

That this Synod recognizing:
(*a*) the urgency of the task of making and preserving peace; and
(*b*) the extreme seriousness of the threat made to the world by contemporary nuclear weapons and the dangers in the present international situation; and
(*c*) that it is not the task of the church to determine defence strategy but rather to give a moral lead to the nation:

  (i) affirms that it is the duty of Her Majesty's Government and her allies to maintain adequate forces to guard against nuclear blackmail and to deter nuclear and non-nuclear aggressors:

  (ii) asserts that the tactics and strategies of this country and her NATO allies should be seen to be unmistakeably defensive in respect of the countries of the Warsaw Pact;

  (iii) judges that even a small-scale first use of nuclear weapons could never be morally justified in view of the high risk that this would lead to full-scale nuclear warfare;

  (iv) believes that there is a moral obligation on all countries (including the members of NATO) publicly to forswear the first use of nuclear weapons in any form;

  (v) bearing in mind that many in Europe live in fear of nuclear catastrophe and that nuclear parity is not essential to deterrence, calls on Her Majesty's Government to take immediate steps in conjunction with her allies to further the principles embodied in this motion so as to reduce progressively NATO's dependence on nuclear weapons and to decrease nuclear arsenals throughout the world.[13]

There appears little basic difference between the official attitude of the two churches on this important subject of nuclear defence.

From this brief consideration of social ethical teaching of the two communions, many similarities will be apparent, and there is happily a general convergence. However, the Church of England as a national church and one which is officially 'established' is concerned with ethical issues which concern the nation as well as the church (the recent report *Faith in the City*[14] of the Archbishop of Canterbury's Commission on Urban Priority Areas is a good example of this). It is often concerned with matters of law (about which its Board for Social Responsibility is often asked to comment), or with proposed changes of law (about which it is also often asked to give evidence to government enquiries). By contrast, the Roman Catholic Church, as a worldwide group of diocesan churches united under the Pope and accepting his universal jurisdiction and magisterium, is more concerned with the church's own distinctive thinking on ethical problems and with the responsibilities of hierarchies and church members.

This happy convergence of ethical attitudes does not, however, apply to all areas of morality.

7

The Church and Sexual Ethics

The major area of difference on matters of morality between the
Roman Catholic and Anglican Churches lies within the field of
sexual ethics. Since the gift of sex finds its proper fulfilment within
marriage, it is at this point that the examination of any differences
should begin. Happily, however, there is no fundamental difference
between the two churches as regards what marriage of its nature is
or the ends which it is ordained to serve. The Roman Catholic-
Anglican International Commission on the Theology of Marriage
reported:

> The language of Vatican II in *Gaudium et Spes* (47–52) grounding
> marriage in the natural order in the mutual pact or covenant
> (pactum, foedus) of the spouses, is entirely at one with the
> convenantal interpretation of marriage written into the Anglican
> liturgies. The sacramental nature of marriage is also affirmed,
> partly in the moral sense of enduring obligation (sacramentum)
> expressed in the marriage vow, partly in the sense of sign
> (signum); a sign to the world of what marriage in the natural
> order by God's ordinance is and ought to be; a sign to the world
> and to the Church of Christ's irrevocable convenant with the
> Church and of the mutual love which finds expression between
> Him and the Church . . .[1]

The International Commission concludes that 'this substantial
convergence in doctrine, despite differences in the language used to

express it, is a welcome fact of our time, too precious to permit us to rest on the polarities suggested by the time-honoured formulations of the Reformation and Counter-Reformation'.[2]

This convergence is a matter of much thanksgiving. Yet there are some differences of doctrine and discipline that need to be examined.

In the first place, Roman Catholic doctrine holds that marriage is indissoluble. Therefore it is not possible for a marriage to end except by the death of one of the spouses (apart from the 'Pauline privilege', permitting dissolution of a marriage between two unbaptized pagans when the pagan party refuses to live with the other after baptism, and also the 'Petrine privilege', by which a marriage between non-Catholics can be dissolved, when one of them becomes a Roman Catholic, providing that at least one party was unbaptized at the time of the marriage). This apparently strict marriage discipline has been, however, much mitigated by the practice of annulment (i.e. a declaration that no valid marriage ever existed). Annulments are of two kinds; impedient (which can be dispensed) and diriment (which make a marriage null from the outset). The development of nullity in recent years by extending its grounds through defective intention, or through an inability to make a proper intention, has further eased the situation. Since the magisterium, focussed in the Bishop of Rome, has, in accordance with Roman Catholic views of authority, the power to grant nullities, a whole tradition of casuistry in this connection has grown up for the use of diocesan curial courts and the exercise of matrimonial jurisdiction in Rome.

By contrast the Church of England does not make use of nullity (which may however exceptionally be recognized in an English court of law). Until the nineteenth century, however, her ecclesiastical courts had jurisdiction for issuing decrees of divorce, and in a number of cases exercised that jurisdiction. Marriage itself is described in Canon Law as follows:

The Church of England affirms, according to our Lord's teaching, that marriage is in its nature a union permanent and life-long, for better or for worse, till death do them part, of one man with one woman, to the exclusion of all others on either side, for the procreation and nurture of children, for the hallowing and right direction of the natural instincts and affections, and for the mutual society, help and comfort which the one ought to have of the other, both in prosperity and in adversity (B 30 I).

At the same time, this Canon does not actually deny the possibility that a marriage may die. In the recent past the Church of England has set up a succession of Commissions to enquire into the nature of marriage and divorce;[3] and although as a result of exhaustive debate the Church of England has not changed its regulations, it has been established that there are within it four valid and differing views about the nature of marriage and divorce; 1. that it is indissoluble, 2. that it is dissoluble but never ought to be dissolved; 3. that it is dissoluble, and although it ought to be permanent in intention, there are occasions when it is proper to dissolve a marriage and to permit remarriage; and 4. that a marriage may die, and in such circumstances it may be right to remarry. The Canon Law of the Church of England makes no mention of divorce or the possibility of remarriage in church or elsewhere; and while remarriage in church is prohibited by a Convocation Regulation, it is permitted by the law of the land, and an increasing number of clergymen, at their own discretion, and as a result of an informed conscience, believe that it is right to make use of their liberty under the law.[4]

There is therefore a different tradition between the Roman Catholic Church in the case of marriage breakdown; one through the use of nullity procedures, and the other by way of the use of a liberty under the law, a way which is not officially approved of by the church, but which at the same time is recognized as appropriate on the part of those clergymen whose consciences are overstretched by the present official regulations. It is difficult to see any way of reconciliation between the two communions on this matter, as traditions have developed along divergent lines.

If there are differences about the permanence of marriage between the two communions, there is an even greater difference over what is euphemistically called 'the use of marriage'. Artificial contraception within marriage is forbidden by the Roman Catholic Church, and welcomed (with the mutual agreement of both partners) within the Anglican Churches.

Here the Anglican Churches have changed their views over the years, and this is best shown by successive Resolutions of Lambeth Conferences. The issue was raised here for the first time in 1920, and that year's Conference in Resolution 70 'urges the importance of enlisting the help of all high-principled men and women whatever their religious beliefs' against, among other things 'the open and secret sale of contraceptives'.[5] The Conference, in Resolution 68, uttered 'an emphatic warning against the use of unnatural means for the avoidance of conception', and the only concession that was made was that the Lambeth Fathers declined 'to lay down rules which will meet the needs of every abnormal case'.[6]

Ten years later, the tone of the Conference had changed. Abstinence was still enjoined for the limitation of families; 'it brings with it to those who claim and receive divine grace the opportunity for the highest exercise of Christian love and self-denial'. Yet the 1930 Lambeth Conference passed Resolution 15:

> Where there is a clearly felt moral obligation to limit and avoid parenthood, the method must be decided on Christian principles. The primary and obvious method is complete abstinence from sexual intercourse (as far as may be necessary) in a life of discipline and self-control lived in the power of the Holy Spirit. Nevertheless in those cases where there is such a clearly felt moral obligation to avoid parenthood, and where there is a morally sound reason for avoiding complete abstinence, the Conference agrees that other methods may be used, provided that this is done in the light of the same Christian principles. The Conference records its strong condemnation of the use of any methods of contraception control from motives of selfishness, luxury or mere convenience.[7]

By 1958 the Lambeth Conference had moved further. The theme of 'The Family in Contemporary Society' had been carefully explored before the conference by a group working under the chairmanship of Canon M. A. C. Warren. The Conference Report included a long section on the subject of family planning; and Resolution 115 reads as follows:

> The Conference believes that the responsibility for deciding upon the number and frequency of children has been laid by God upon the consciences of parents everywhere; and this planning, in such ways as are mutually acceptable to husband and wife in Christian conscience, is a right and important factor in Christian family life and should be the result of positive choice before God. Such

responsible parenthood, built on obedience to all the duties of marriage, requires a wise stewardship of the resources and abilities of the family as well as a thoughtful consideration of the varying population needs and the claims of future generations.[8]

The advent of the 'pill', or control of a woman's fertility by the oral administration of hormones, gave a new urgency to the attitude of the Roman Catholic Church on artificial contraception. Pope Paul VI accepted that the discovery by man of new methods of control over reproduction, together with the 'population explosion' in the developing world, had given rise to new questions. He set up a Commission, consisting of married couples as well as men, who were expert in various related fields, to provide the magisterium with evidence in which to give an apt reply to these questions, and he also consulted his fellow Roman Catholic Bishops. His own response was given in *Humanae Vitae*:

> The Church, in urging men to the observance of the precepts of the natural law, which it interprets by its constant doctrine, teaches as absolutely required that *in any use whatever of marriage* there must be no impairment of its natural capacity to procreate human life.[9]

The Roman Catholic Church accepts the principle of double effect, that is to say, providing that the purpose of an action is proper and legitimate, its secondary effect is also acceptable, and therefore 'the Church regards it in no way unlawful to use means considered necessary to cure diseases, even though they have also a contraceptive effect, and this is foreseen, provided that this contraceptive effect is not directly intended for any motive whatsoever'.[10]

The reasoning behind the different approaches of the two communions is as different as the methods by which they reach them. The 1920 Lambeth Fathers were against 'artificial contraceptives' because they believed that these encouraged the deliberate cultivation of sexual union as an end in itself; and that the use of contraceptives is unnatural in that it prevents the primary aim of marriage, the procreation of children. The 1930 Lambeth Conference speaks somewhat vaguely of 'moral situations' which make it necessary to use artificial contraceptives rather than the way of abstinence; and notes that no direction on the subject has been given by an ecumenical council. 'It can never be right for intercourse to take place which might lead to conception, where a birth might involve grave danger to health, even to the life of the mother, or where a birth would inflict upon the child to be born a life of suffering . . .'[11] The 1958 Report is much more positive about married intercourse:

> The procreation of children is not the only purpose of marriage . . . Sexual intercourse is not the only language of earthly love, but it is, in its right and full use, the most intimate and revealing . . . It is a giving and receiving in the unity of two free spirits which is in itself good (within the marriage bond) and mediates good to those who share it. Therefore it is utterly wrong to urge that, unless children are specifically desired, sexual intercourse is of the nature of sin. It is also wrong to say that such intercourse ought not to be engaged in except with the willing intention to procreate children.[12]

By contrast, the Roman Catholic encyclical states unequivocally that it is wrong to think that a whole married life of otherwise normal relations can justify sexual intercourse which is deliberately contraceptive and so intrinsically wrong.[13] It is intrinsically wrong because it is the natural result of such intercourse to create life (as well as to unite the married couple in love) and to impair that natural capacity so as to prevent procreation by whatever means is contrary to natural law, and therefore contrary to God's will. Because artificial contraceptives break the natural law, they should never deliberately be used to prevent conception. (Others might quarrel with this application of the natural law; but that is the argument of the encyclical.)

Is there any possible meeting point between the two different viewpoints of the Anglican and Roman Catholic Churches? Both I think accept the same principles but interpret them differently. Thus Pope Paul VI asks: 'Could it not be admitted that procreative finality applies to the whole of married life rather than to each act?'[14] This is a coded question which asks whether each and every act of intercourse must be open to procreation providing that, in the marriage as a whole, there is an intention to have children as well as to strengthen the union through intercourse. Unfortunately the Pope did not explain the reasons for his negative response to this question which he has asked himself. Professor O'Donovan puts the contrast with the Anglican attitude well:

To break marriage down into a series of disconnected acts is to
falsify its true nature. As a whole, then, the married love of any
couple (barring serious reasons to the contrary) should be both
relation-building and procreative; the two ends of marriage are
held together in the life of sexual partnership which the couple live
together . . . What was at issue in the matter of contraception was
not the unity of procreation and unity as such, but the Moral
Theological tradition known as 'strict analysis' which tends, in the
eyes of critics, to atomize certain human activities in ways that defy
their inner structure.[15]

It seems then that the Roman Catholic attitude could be altered with
integrity not by the surrender of some basic theological principle, but
by the use of a different moral theological principle than that of 'strict
analysis'. The Anglican viewpoint changed between 1920 and 1958
by the consideration of further factors which had not previously been
considered (e.g. the unitive aspect of married intercourse), and there
is a possibility of further change for the Roman Catholic viewpoint as
indicated above.

Abortion is another subject which presently divides the Roman
Catholic Church and the Anglican Church. However, the grounds of
this division are not usually well understood. For example, it is often
taken for granted that the official Roman Catholic position is that the
human person is present from the moment of conception onwards;
and that therefore all human embryos and foetuses are sacred. But
this is not the case, according to the latest Declaration on Abortion by
the Sacred Congregation of the Faith on 18 November 1974.

In this Declaration it is acknowledged that in the Middle Ages it
was commonly thought that the spiritual soul was present in the
foetus only after the first two weeks. In fact this view derives from the
Greek version of Ex. 21.22, according to which the penalty levied for
a personal injury that leads to spontaneous abortion was mitigated if
the foetus was 'unformed'. The Greek text influenced the Greek
fathers, and through them Augustine and St Thomas Aquinas who
held, after Aristotle, that conception was not completed until the
eightieth day. However, this view was questioned, especially in the
last century as the evils of abortion increased. The Roman Catholic
Declaration stated in 1974:

This Declaration deliberately leaves aside at what moment in time
the spiritual soul is infused. On this matter tradition is not unanim-

ous, and writers differ. Some assert it happens at the first instance of life, while others consider that it does not happen before the seed has taken up its position.

The Declaration points out that from the moment of conception the embryo has its own fixed genetic programme enabling it to develop into a particular human being with certain characteristics; but it may not be as yet a human being. Indeed:

> It is not within the competence of biology to adjudicate on matters which are strictly philosophical and ethical, such as the question when a human person is constituted or the legitimacy of abortion.[16]

The point is pressed, for the Declaration goes on to say: 'It is not for science to resolve such questions, since the existence of an immortal soul is not within its competence. The question is a philosophical one . . .' Because a philosophical view can never be absolutely certain (in contrast, according to the Roman Catholic view, to a divine revelation on the matter), it follows that an abortion involves the risk of killing an ensouled embryo or an ensouled foetus. On the principle of tutiorism (e.g. the safer solution is the right one), abortion must be wrong. 'It is certain that, even if one were to doubt whether the result of conception is already a human person, it is objectively a serious sin to incur the risk of committing homicide.' The question is also answered in somewhat different terms: 'If the infusion of the soul is judged only as probable (for the contrary will never be certain) to take its life is the same as incurring the *danger* of killing not just what it is hoped will be a man, but what is a man certainly possessed of a soul.'

The Roman Catholic view about abortion is thus based on 1. the view that if a foetus in ensouled, its abortion is murder; 2. the decision about when a foetus is ensouled is a philosophical one; and 3. it is morally wrong to take the risk that it is not ensouled, since no certainty can be achieved.

Whatever be the philosophical and theological base upon which it rests, the Roman Catholic official view against abortion has been very strongly held. For a time the 'absolutist' position gained the ascendency, and in decrees of the Holy Office of 28 May 1884, 19 August 1889 and 5 May 1902 actions which might be taken to save a mother's life by foeticide were explicitly condemned. These decrees, however, were so repugnant to conscience that a way was found round them by the exercise of casuistry. A further decree of 4 May 1898, stating that in every premature delivery, every effort must be made to save the life of both mother and child, was interpreted by the law of double effect to mean that every effort could be made to save the mother's life when the child she was bearing could never be delivered as a normal living child.[17] So sanity prevailed!

The Anglican viewpoint on abortion, and the method of arriving at it, has been very different.

Little action was taken before the middle of this century. Abortion was generally held to be wrong, and it was forbidden by the law of the land, and the subject was not discussed in either secular or ecclesiastical circles. However, before the passing of the Abortion Act 1967, there was much public discussion and the Board for Social Responsibility set up a committee under Canon I. T. Ramsey (afterwards Bishop of Durham) which produced a report *Abortion – An Ethical Discussion* in 1965. In this Report, it was concluded that it was not helpful to argue from the question whether the foetus is a human being or not; and that similar difficulties attended discussion about 'soul', 'life' and 'person' in this connection. 'The choice will inevitably be influenced by the evaluative conclusions that we want to come to.'[18] And so the Committee adopted another method of arguing. Its basic presumption was that a foetus, although not a typical adult human being, has a potential future of becoming one, and so its life should be preserved unless it can be argued, on one of a number of grounds, that it would have been better had that child not been born. The particular cases examined by the committee in which this could be the case were 1. those in which a pregnancy constitutes a grave threat to the mother's life or health, 2. those in which there is a calculable risk of the birth of a deformed or defective child and 3. those in which a child has been conceived as a result of rape or some other criminal offence.

As a result of this Report, the Church Assembly resolved in February 1966 that

The Assembly welcomes the Report: *Abortion – An Ethical Discussion* because it stresses the principle of the sanctity of life for mother and foetus and urges the Church to preserve and demonstrate a balance between compassion for the mother and a proper responsibility for the life of the unborn child, and instructs the Board for Social Responsibility to continue its study of this subject.[19]

The General Synod has returned to the subject of abortion no less than four times, because of the unsatisfactory working of the Abortion Act 1967, and in July 1983 resolved that this Synod:

(a) believes that all human life, including life developing in the womb, is created by God in his own image and is, therefore, to be nurtured supported and protected;

(b) views with serious concern the number and consequences of abortions performed in the United Kingdom in recent years;

(c) recognizes that in situations where the continuance of a pregnancy threatens the life of the mother a termination of pregnancy may be justified and that there must be safe and adequate provision in our society for such situations . . .[20]

The Church of England has within its membership those who hold the 'absolutist' position which has been officially adopted by the Roman Catholic Church; but in its official pronouncements it has modified that position to justify a termination of pregnancy in certain carefully defined cases for the sake of the mother. This viewpoint has been arrived at not by means of decrees of the magisterium, but after public debate which has included open discussion by lay men and women who have participated in the decision-making process. Is there any way in which the two churches can be reconciled in this matter? Perhaps there might be an extension of the casuistry on the part of the Roman Catholic Church which modified the decisions of the decrees of 1884, 19 August 1889, and 1902 so as to bring their present position into line with the Anglican position, which itself could well be strengthened by greater precision.

The Warnock Report or more properly *The Report of the Committee of Inquiry into Human Fertilization and Embryology*[21] which was published in 1984 has raised some issues akin to those involved in our consideration of abortion, as well as others concerned with procreation and the exclusive nature of marriage. Modern medical techniques have made children possible for those couples who cannot have them (or who ought not to have them) by reason of some physical disability suffered by one or both partners. These comprise artificial insemination by husband (AIH), artificial insemination by donor (AID), in vitro fertilization, egg donation, embryo donation and surrogacy. The Committee also considered the wider use of these techniques, and examined the question of research into human embryos.

The Roman Catholic Bishops' Conference of England and Wales made two submissions to the Warnock Committee; one from its Social Welfare Commission (*Human Fertilization – Choices for the Future*) and the other from the Joint Committee on Bio-Ethical Issues on behalf of the Catholic Bishops of Great Britain (*In Vitro Fertilization – Morality and Public Policy*). The former is more concerned with social consequences than with fundamental ethics, and it is the latter which concerns us here. The main objection that the Commission had against in vitro fertilization and against donation of genetic material is best expressed in its own words:

> To choose to have a child by IVF is to choose to have a child as the product of a making. But the relationship of product to maker is a relationship of radical inequality, of profound insubordination. Thus the choice to have or to create a child does not have the status which the child of sexual union has, a status which is a great good for any child: the status of radical equality with parents, as partner like them in the familial community.
>
> In that choice, and in his or her life thereafter, the IVF child is also deprived of the *identity* of self-understanding of other children who can (in effect) say of themselves: 'I had my origin in a single act, an act of love or friendship or mutual involvement and commitment, an act *equally of each of my parents* and of them alone; an act by which they submitted themselves to each other and to the source of human life.[22]

This viewpoint is shared by many Anglicans, who, even for such a good as to enable a family to be fruitful, believe that the techniques of embryo donation, egg donation and AIH are unacceptable. Some also believe that to import alien genetic material (from either male or female) breaks the exclusive nature of the marriage covenant, to say nothing of the effect of such origins on the children born as a result of any of these techniques.

The Church of England submitted evidence to the Warnock Committee and also published its response to the Warnock Report.[23] Furthermore, its Board for Social Responsibility set up a Working Group among its members which produced a report *Personal Origins*,[24] for more general consideration by those not skilled in these matters. These reports admitted that its members were divided on these matters although the majority was in favour of the conditional use of these new techniques, except for embryo donation; and all were unanimously against surrogacy agreements, as cheapening the role of women in bearing children, as well as preventing a mother from nurturing the child she has carried in her womb.

The Anglican reports also commented on proposals to control by law research on human embryos (at the moment of writing there are no legal controls). There are those who object to this research, despite the great good that might come from it, by the eradication of some genetically inherited disability, and by a greater knowledge of embryo development which could be therapeutically useful. The division of opinion and convictions in these matters stem from differing views about the status of the human embryo. If it is regarded as a human person, the rights inhering in human personhood belong to a human embryo, and any experiment would be immoral because consent is impossible. Views differ on this matter. Some hold that God infuses a human embryo with a soul at the moment of conception, and would resist experimentation for that reason; and similarly those who stress the continuity of the human being from the moment of conception. Others, noting that until the embryo is implanted in the womb it cannot survive, and that the 'primitive streak' develops some fourteen days after conception, and that twinning may take place and (under laboratory conditions of IVF) recombination can also occur within this period, hold that licensed experimentation for the good of humanity should be permitted for fourteen days after conception. Others would extend permission until the first beginnings of the sensory system develop twenty-one days after conception. For these people the language of 'God infusing a soul into the human embryo' is unsatisfactory. They prefer to think in the same terms as the well-known Roman Catholic ethicist John Mahoney:

As in the case of life itself originating from inorganic matter, so in the case of human emergence within the evolutionary process and in the case of each human reproduction what is involved may be not so much God's 'by-passing' his creatures to intervene 'immediately' by injecting a new miracle ingredient and in the case of man, 'pouring' in a human soul, but rather new states of being 'welling up' from within, through the genuine activity of created agencies (whether inorganic or humanoid or human) which have already reached a certain threshold of existence and are impelled further by the cosmic creative activity of God.[25]

Despite this speculation by a distinguished Roman Catholic ethicist, official Roman Catholicism is of course opposed to embryo experimentation. Anglicans are deeply divided on this, as on other proposals of the Warnock Committee. The first time that General Synod voted on these matters in November 1984, general approval of the proposals was witheld by a narrow margin of votes: when a second vote on a similar motion was taken in June 1985, approval was given also by a narrow margin. As yet Anglican opinion has not had time to crystallize; and the way is not clear for a settled and lasting decision. The techniques are new, and the evaluation of them in ethical terms is difficult and as yet unclear. Perhaps by contrast with Roman Catholicism, Anglicanism is not afraid of admitting continuing perplexity over difficult moral matters, and, as new factors come to light, is willing to acknowledge possible development in its ethical judgments.

Both communions have also concerned themselves with the morality of relationships between people of the same sex. The Roman Catholic Sacred Congregation of the Faith published *Sexual Ethics*, a Declaration on certain questions relating to sexual matters. One of these matters concerns homosexual relations, although only one page is devoted to the subject. The Declaration makes a distinction between habituated homosexuals and those who are homosexual by nature. Homosexual acts are condemned in the Declaration on objective grounds, because they 'lack an essential and indispensable finality'. (This phrase is not explained in the Declaration, but presumably the meaning intended is that they cannot lead to the procreation of children; in so far as such acts may deepen a permanent personal relationship, they could be said to have a certain finality.) The Declaration confirms that such acts are intrinsically disordered and can in no case be approved of. Certainly the Declaration affirms that the culpability of such couples must 'be judged with prudence', but it goes on to declare: 'No pastoral method can be employed which would give moral justification on the grounds that they would be consonant with the condition of such people.'[26]

The Church of England by contrast has dealt with this question at much greater length, and with less tangible result. The Board for Social Responsibility set up in 1974 a Working Party under the Rt Revd John Yates, the Bishop of Gloucester, to study the theological, social, pastoral and legal aspects of homosexuality. The Working Party's Report, which was published in 1979, and which took into account earlier Anglican thinking on these matters, deeply divided the Board which took the unprecedented step, after ten month's discussion, of including with the Report its own critical observations.[27] There ensued a debate in the General Synod in February 1981, in which the tone was set by Dr Runcie, Archbishop of Canterbury, who suggested that homosexuality should be seen 'not as a sin or as a sickness but more as a handicap'.[28] At the end of a long and serious debate, a motion was put both welcoming the Board's Report (containing the Working Party's Report and its own Observations) but dissociating itself from the Working Party's Report. A procedural motion was then put and carried, that 'the House do pass to next business'. In other words, the Church of England refused to make an official pronouncement either negative or positive, on the subject of homosexuality. There is a sense in which it referred the questions concerning homosexuality to the private judgment of its members. This might at first sight appear to be a sign of weakness and division. It is however worth noting some words of the Rt Revd Graham Leonard, then Chairman of the Board for Social Responsibility:

I think that we have got to have the patience to wait until the Church resolves this matter, and I think that we have made it clear in the debate today that in waiting and listening and debating we are not abdicating our responsibility for speaking in the name of the Lord on moral issues to our nation . . .

The Bishop admitted that we have not worked out fully in the Church of England questions of authority in personal ethics, or of the magisterium, to use the phrase more customary in the Roman Catholic Church. The Bishop instanced as a parallel the long period of debate which preceded the definition of the person of Christ at Chalcedon as an example of the time in which it takes the church to make up its mind on controverted matters. It could be said (and indeed I would say) that it is a strength of Anglicanism to weigh new insights into truth, and to live with controversy and conflict until a consensus is given which enables an authoritative statement to be made. Certainly, as Bishop Leonard remarked: 'There is no question of this Synod, as representing the Church of England, saying that anything goes.'[29]

Is there any possibility of reconciling the two churches on this matter? In a sense the future lies open, since the Church of England *might* at some time in the future pronounce on the matter in agreement with the Roman Catholic Declaration. At the same time, perhaps in future a distinction could be made between moral and pastoral theology. Moral theology has as its task the discovery of what actions are objectively right, in so far as a judgment can be made. Pastoral theology might have the task of applying these principles to actual pastoral situations. It can never be the case that it is right to do something that is objectively wrong for its own sake; but it is possible to make a choice between two courses of action, both of which diminish human personality and fall short of what is good; and it is at least conceivable that in such circumstances that which is morally (or objectively) wrong could be justified on pastoral grounds.

It is not without interest that the Roman Catholic Declaration devoted twice as much space to masturbation as it did to homosexuality; whereas the Church of England has never considered this matter officially at all. The Declaration states:

> Both the Magisterium of the Church – in the course of a constant tradition – and the moral sense of the faithful have declared without hesitation that masturbation is an intrinsically and seriously disordered act. The main reason is that, whatever the motive for acting in this way, the deliberate use of the sexual faculty outside normal conjugal relations essentially contradicts the finality of the faculty.[30]

The Declaration also speaks of 'solitary pleasure closed in on self', and even invokes here the concept of 'mortal sin'. By contrast the Church of England has been entirely silent on the matter, possibly due to its tradition of voluntary rather than compulsory celibacy. Could there be a reconciliation here of the two communions? Of course it is possible that the Church of England might come into line with the official view of the Roman Catholic Church, although I think that this is unlikely; and once again a distinction could be made between moral and pastoral theology in this matter as in abortion.

The Declaration on Sexual Ethics does not mention sterilization but the Encyclical *Humanae Vitae* explicitly condemns it, whether of the man or of the woman, whether permanent or temporary.[31] By contrast the Lambeth Conference of the Anglican Communion, meeting in 1958, discussed the matter in one of its committees, and while not condemning it absolutely pointed out that it involved a violation of the human body and should only be chosen after the deepest and gravest thought, with full agreement between the spouses. The Church of England's Board for Social Responsibility later set up an ethical enquiry under the chairmanship of the late Dr R. C. Mortimer, then Bishop of Exeter. The Committee concluded:

> Faced as we are by a situation in which a responsible government is pursuing, together with other ameliorative measures, a policy of persuasion for voluntary sterilization, and asked by Christian doctors and nurses involved in the carrying out of this policy for help in deciding for themselves how far they can co-operate, we are bound to conclude that we find no grounds on which to reply in terms of an absolute negative. The Church of England does not claim to be infallible, and it may err. But it does believe in progressive revelation under the guidance of the Holy Spirit. And we believe that light on this question is slowly dawning, and we are prepared tentatively to express the opinion that there are circumstances in which an operation for sterilization may legitimately be employed.[32]

Here is another divergence in sexual ethics between the Roman Catholic and the Anglican Churches, although it must be stressed that this particular report was produced before the General Synod came into existence, and cannot be said to have full authority within the Church of England.

The differences in sexual ethics between the two churches is very considerable. These differences were to some extent highlighted by an attempt by a private member of General Synod in 1979 to get the Synod to welcome the Roman Catholic Declaration as 'a necessary and compassionate statement of traditional Christian teaching'. This met with little success in what the Rt Revd Dr Habgood called 'a perfectly dreadful debate'.[33] One somewhat hostile speaker quoted from a 1976 issue of the Roman Catholic *Clergy Review* about the failure in Rome to get a Declaration which did justice both to a personalist and a traditional approach.[34] An attempt to 'pass to next business' failed on a technicality. Anglicans wanted to be courteous to their Roman Catholic brothers and sisters; but nonetheless the motion suffered the ultimate indignity of being talked out when it was discovered that there was not present a quorum from the House of Bishops!

The Roman Catholic Church maintains the discipline of its teaching on sexual ethics through the operation of its magisterium. For example, the teaching of the Revd Charles Curran of the Catholic University in Washington (whose views on these matters approximate to the Anglican position) is currently causing conflict between himself and the Sacred Congregation of the Faith, and his future is in doubt.

Despite these differences between the Church of England and the Roman Catholic Church, there is happily a very large area of agreement in sexual ethics, not only about the nature of love and marriage but also on the calling of all to chastity, whether celibate or married, as well as on the sins of fornication and adultery. It is not impossible that the two churches will at some time agree over matters of sexual ethics; and there is good reason to look forward to them moving closer together with the same tendency to convergence as has been noted in the area of dogmatics. The Roman Catholic Sacred Congregation for the Doctrine of the Faith did, however, in its *Observations* on the Final ARCIC Report, comment that 'since the dialogue has as its final objective the restoration of church unity, it will necessarily have to be extended to all points which constitute an obstacle to that unity. Among these points it will be appropriate to give moral teaching an important place'.[35] Such an examination has been lacking hitherto; and it is hoped to be that these two chapters on the theme will help towards a more detailed consideration.

8

Women and the
Ministerial Priesthood

In November 1962 the Church Assembly of the Church of England
(the precursor of the General Synod) passed a resolution asking the
Archbishops to set up a Committee to make a thorough examination of the various reasons 'for the withholding of the ordained and
representative ministry from women'. This request arose from a
report from the Church's Advisory Council for the Training of the
Ministry which had recommended an enquiry into 'reasons theological, traditional, instinctive, anthropological, social, emotional'
which resulted in women being excluded from the ordained
ministry.[1]

The report *Women and Holy Orders*[2] was introduced into the
Church Assembly by the Rt Revd Gerald Ellison (later Bishop of
London), in 1967. This marked the beginning of serious interest
within the Church of England in women's ordination; but opinion
was deeply divided, so divided that the Church Assembly was
unable to pass any motion whatsoever in connection with the
Report! The 1968 Lambeth Conference resolved as follows:

> The Conference affirms its opinion that the theological argu-
> ments as at present presented for and against the ordination of
> women are inconclusive.[3]

Each national or regional Church or Province was asked to study
the question and to report its findings to the Anglican Consultative
Council.

When the Council met in 1971 it found itself faced not merely with the results of these studies by constituent churches, but also by a specific request. The Anglican Church of Hong Kong and Macao wanted to know whether or not to proceed to the ordination of women forthwith.

Already a woman had been ordained to the priesthood within that church. Lee Tim Oi had been ordained deacon in 1941. In the very difficult pastoral situation caused by the Japanese occupation of Hong Kong and Macao, she had exceptionally been granted a license as a deacon to celebrate the holy communion. Bishop R. O. Hall, when he found out about this situation, judged that it was more consonant with church order to ordain her to the priesthood. (His action was repudiated by the Archbishops of Canterbury and York as soon as they heard of it, and Lee Tim Oi ceased to exercise her Orders, living in South China until the cultural revolution in 1966.)

The Anglican Church of Hong Kong was later consulted by Bishop Hall's successor about the ordination of women to the priesthood with reference to women deacons already well known in that diocese. After a very thorough discussion by parishes, the diocesan synod decided by an overwhelming majority that it would be right to ordain women to the priesthood. Bishop Baker remitted the matter to the Anglican Consultative Council, meeting in Kenya in 1971, for its advice. The Council decided, by a small majority, that if the diocese of Hong Kong did proceed to ordain women, this would be acceptable, and that all Provinces and regional Councils of the Anglican Communion should be encouraged to remain in communion with the diocese. On 28 November 1971 the first two women in the Anglican Communion, after due synodical process, were validly ordained to the priesthood; and no Province or Council of the Anglican Communion broke off communion with that diocese.

The Anglican Consultative Council, when it had met in Kenya in 1971, had asked the churches of the Anglican Communion to express their views on the ordination of women in time for their meeting in 1973. In fact the Church of England did not move until later, inviting the opinions of the dioceses in 1973 and debating in General Synod in 1975 the motion that 'in the opinion of this Synod there are no fundamental objections to the ordination of women to the priesthood'. This motion was passed in the three Houses of

Bishops, Clergy and Laity, but not by large majorities (except for the House of Bishops).

Elsewhere in the Anglican Communion women began to be ordained to the priesthood, some after due synodical process (as in the Church of Canada), some irregularly at first, but later regularized with further ordinations authorized (in the Episcopal Church of the USA). In 1978 the Bishops of the Anglican Communion met for the Lambeth Conference. The ordination of women to the priesthood dominated the Conference, for feelings had run high, both among those convinced that women should be ordained to the priesthood, and those who believed that such ordinations were contrary to God's will, or that the Anglican Communion had no authority to alter catholic order. The Conference was in fact crucial for the future of the Anglican Communion.

Resolution 21 recognized the autonomy of each constituent church to make its own decisions, but it also emphasized the importance of such a decision to the other churches; and the Conference affirmed its commitment to the preservation of unity within and between all member churches of the Communion.

The Conference therefore encouraged all the member churches to continue in communion with one another, notwithstanding the fact that some had ordained women to the presbyterate. Recognizing that there might be problems of conscience, it urged that 'every action be taken to ensure that all baptized members of the church continued to be in communion with their bishop and that every opportunity be given for all members to work together in the mission of the church irrespective of their convictions regarding this issue.'

The Anglican Consultative Council was requested to use its good offices between those member churches which ordained women and those which did not, and to maintain and as far as possible to extend the present dialogue with churches outside the Anglican family. (The Anglican Communion was not only in dialogue with the Roman Catholic Church, but also with the Orthodox Churches.)

The Conference agreed a policy of 'live and let live'. In three clauses the Conference:

(a) declared its acceptance of those member Churches which now ordain women, and urged that they respect the convictions of those provinces and dioceses which do not;

(b) declared its acceptance of those member Churches which do not ordain women and urges that they respect the convictions of those provinces and dioceses which do;

(c) with regard to women who have been ordained in the Anglican Communion being authorized to exercise their ministry in Provinces which have not ordained women, recommended that should synodical authority be given them to exercise it, it should be exercised only

  (i) where pastoral need warrants and

  (ii) where such a ministry is agreeable to the bishop, clergy and people where the ministry is to be exercised . . .

The Lambeth Conference recognized that such a variety of doctrine and practice might be disappointing to other churches in the Catholic tradition, but it justified its stance on the grounds that the holding together of a diversity within a unity of faith is part of the Anglican heritage. It emphasized that those churches which had ordained women to the priesthood believed that these ordinations had been into the historic ministry of the church as the Anglican Communion had received it, and it hoped that dialogue with these other churches would continue because there was still much to learn from them about the understanding of the truth of God, as all moved towards a fuller catholicity and a deeper fellowship in the Holy Spirit. Furthermore it was agreed that no woman be ordained to the episcopate without overwhelming support in any member church and in the diocese concerned, and after consultation with the episcopate through the Primates.

Meanwhile the question of women's ordination to the priesthood was causing increasing agitation within the Church of England, especially in the more catholic wing of that Church (but also among Evangelicals who held from the scriptures that women should not be in a position of ecclesiastical authority): and a voluminous literature appeared.[4] In 1978 the General Synod of the Church of England debated all day the motion:

That this Synod asks the Standing Committee to prepare and bring forward legislation to remove the barriers to the ordination of women to the priesthood and their consecration to the episcopate.

I moved this motion, and it was opposed by the Rt Revd Graham Leonard, then Bishop of Truro. It would be inappropriate to reproduce in the body of this book the arguments deployed on either side; but they are reproduced in an appendix. The motion was decisively lost both in the House of Clergy and in the House of Laity (although decisively won in the House of Bishops). Since 1978 the argument has continued within the Church of England, and feeling has run high. A Measure to ordain Deaconesses as Deacons has passed through all its stages in General Synod and (at the time of writing) awaits parliamentary approval. A carefully guarded Measure enabling women validly ordained abroad to minister in a parish of the Church of England for a limited period is at present going through the synodical process and has not (at the time of writing) yet had to cross the hurdle of a two-thirds majority vote, while ahead lies still another trial of strength over the ordination of women to the priesthood in the Church of England. For General Synod returned to the subject in November 1984 when a motion which originated in a Deanery Synod was brought to General Synod from the Southwark Diocesan Synod. The terms of the motion were 'that this Synod asks the Standing Committee to bring forward legislation to permit the ordination of women to the priesthood in the Provinces of Canterbury and York'. After an all-day debate, this motion was easily passed by simple majority in all three Houses of Bishops, Clergy and Laity. However, if legislation is to be passed, a two-thirds majority will be needed, which the motion failed to achieve in the Houses of Clergy and Laity.

Nonetheless, the passing of the motion caused real disquiet among its opponents. Threats of schism have been made (and a few clergy and lay persons have left the Church of England). The Rt Revd Graham Leonard, now Bishop of London, has assumed the role of a kind of Archbishop Lefèbvre of the Church of England. He has said that, if women are ordained in the Church of England, he would be prepared to serve and give leadership in a continuing Church of England side by side a church which validly ordained women – in fact in a schism. Anglican history, however, suggests that threats of schism (which are not infrequently made in a church embracing different viewpoints) very seldom result in an actual schism; the Non-jurors, and perhaps the Methodist Church are among the few instances of Anglican schism since the Reformation.

Meanwhile, what was happening in the Roman Catholic Church? The Anglican proponents of women's ordination to the priesthood were not without their sympathizers and supporters within the

Roman Catholic Church, not least in the USA and in Holland. Disquiet about this was felt in Rome to such an extent that in October 1976 Pope Paul VI confirmed a *Declaration on the Question of the Admission of Women to the Ministerial Priesthood*, although the statement was not in fact published until 1977.[5] In its introduction the Declaration stated that 'the Sacred Congregation for the Doctrine of the Faith judges it necessary to recall that the Church, in fidelity to the example of the Lord, does not consider herself authorized to admit women to priestly ordination'.

The argument of the Declaration falls into six parts. In the first place it declares that it has been the Church's constant tradition not to ordain women: indeed 'the Church's tradition in the matter has been so firm in the course of the centuries that the magisterium has not felt that the need to intervene in order to formulate a principle which was not attacked, or to defend a law which was not challenged'. On this point the Roman Catholic periodical *The Month* (the organ of the Jesuits) commented: 'As the 1968 Lambeth Conference pointed out, "the New Testament does not encourage Christians to think that nothing should be done for the first time".'[6] The second argument of the Declaration is concerned with the views of Christ, whose attitude to women was quite different from those of his milieu, and yet who did not entrust his apostolic charge to any of them, not even to his own mother. He did not call a woman to be a member of the Twelve. The Declaration sees this to be significant, especially as Jesus' attitude to women was unorthodox for his time.

The third argument of the Declaration focusses on the practice of the apostles. Unlike the Hellenistic world in which the gospel flourished, the church has no priestesses. Women might exercise an important influence in the church by their ministry in bringing people to Christ; e.g. Priscilla, Lydia and Phoebe; but there was no question of conferring ordination upon them. The question arises whether the absence of women's ordination was the result of cultural forces or had a deeper significance. The Declaration sees permanent value in the embargo. It is impossible to *prove* whether it had this deeper significance or not. 'It is, in the last resort, the Church, through the voice of her magisterium, according to Roman Catholic teaching, which decides what can change and what must remain immutable.'[7] According to the Declaration, the unbroken tradition of the catholic church in ordaining only men has a normative value. By contrast, the editorial in *The Month* points out that, if the Holy Spirit can lead us into all truth, this leaves open the possibility of change.[8]

The main argument of the Declaration appears in the fifth section. Christian priesthood is said to be of a sacramental nature. Because it is a sign, it is not merely effectual by divine grace, but it needs to be visible to Christians. The Declaration quotes with approval from the Angelic Doctor. 'Sacramental signs', says St Thomas, 'represent what they signify by natural resemblance.'[9] The argument of *The Month* deserves here to be cited in full:

> The same natural resemblance is required for persons as for things: when Christ's role in the eucharist is to be expressed sacramentally, there would not be this 'natural resemblance' which must exist between Christ and his minister if the role of Christ were not taken by a man: in such a case it would be difficult to see in the minister the image of Christ. For Christ himself was and remains a man.[10]

The Declaration goes on to point out the importance of gender in the scriptural images of bridegroom and bride. If the priest represents Christ, it must be asserted that he first represents Christ, who is the head and the shepherd of the church:

> The second Vatican Council used this phrase to make more precise and to complete the expression *in persona Christi*. It is in this quality that the priest presides over the Christian assembly and celebrates the eucharistic sacrifice 'in which the whole Church offers and is herself wholly offered'.[11]

A similar kind of claim is made in *Sacerdotium Ministeriale* (1983) by the Sacred Congregation of the Faith:

> He (Our Lord) so configures them to himself, that, when they pronounce the words of consecration, they do not act on a mandate from the Community but '*in persona Christi*' which means more than just 'in the name of Christ' or 'in the place of Christ' since the celebrant, by reason of this special sacrament (of Orders) identifies himself with the Eternal High Priest, who is both author and principal agent of his own sacrifice in which truly no one can take his place.[12]

Here again it is pertinent to quote the Editor of *The Month* for a
different Roman Catholic interpretation:

> It is not Christian belief that the priest at the altar *impersonates*
> Jesus of Nazareth; rather he *represents* our redeemer in cele-
> brating the sacrament of our redemption, and, in his saving
> significance, it seems fair to suggest that Christ's masculinity is
> irrelevant. What is important is the humanity which men and
> women share. There may be good pastoral reasons why a change
> overnight would confuse the sign value of the priesthood (for one
> thing we have lived for a long time with the concept of the priest
> as father, though the character of Jesus had more of the brother
> than the father about it). But this is not a theological argument.
> The question is whether we are quite sure to what the sign
> legitimately attaches. There is no doctrine of the church in which
> the fact that Jesus was a man rather than a woman would seem to
> be significant.[13]

It will be seen from these comments that the Declaration has not
met with agreement in some influential Roman Catholic circles;[14]
although of course, like other declarations from the Sacred
Congregation of the Faith, it has authority as coming from the
magisterium of the church. The argument of the Declaration is not
merely that male ordination is the constant tradition of the church,
but also that there are good theological reasons why it should always
remain so. It is the latter point which is contested on grounds of
theology (as well as accepted in practice out of obedience) by some
Roman Catholics (as well as by some Anglicans).

In fact the main theological assault on the position taken up by
the Declaration has come not from a Roman Catholic but from an
Anglican source. Although the argument has been put forward by
an Anglican, it is entirely derived from Roman Catholic sources,
and could just as well (if not better) be deployed within that church
rather than from the Church of England.

John Austin Baker (at present Bishop of Salisbury) has written
about the eucharistic presidency with reference to the nature of the
eucharistic sacrifice. He describes the latter as follows:

> What the celebrant does is to ask God the Father by the power of
> the Holy Spirit to make Christ and his sacrifice present in the
> bread and the wine which are themselves the gift to us of the

Father's love in creation. Everything is done by God the holy Trinity; and above all the sacrifice is performed totally by Christ, because it is his self-offering on Calvary to the Father which is made present among us – not anything at all that we do. The place, if we may use that word, in which his offering of himself becomes real here and now is in the bread and the wine on the altar. It is by eating and drinking these that Christ's body and blood are received. As a consequence, the liturgical action itself is also described as a sacrifice . . . It is true the sacrifice which the priest 'offers' liturgically to God, the ritual act, is understood as worthy only because the heart and substance of it, the offering that is made, is the one perfect sacrifice completed by our Lord outside Jerusalem 1,950 years ago, and which itself represented in earthly terms the perfect love and devotion of the eternal Son to the Father within the Holy Trinity.[15]

This is a straightforward exposition of the doctrine of the eucharistic sacrifice as it is understood in catholic Christendom. The sacrifice of the eucharist is the sacramental representation of the one perfect and sufficient sacrifice which Christ made for the sins of the whole world. But the consequences of this doctrine are not what catholic Christendom has always implied, so far as the ordination of women is concerned. Bishop John Austin Baker continues:

The question, therefore, needs to be pressed: Why, on this understanding of the eucharist, does the celebrant have to be a man? Surely all that is necessary is that the priest should be an officially appointed representative of the Church?[16]

Bishop Baker goes on to explain that the argument for the necessity of a male representative does not draw on this central theology of eucharistic sacrifice so much as on a secondary elaboration of it, which has grown up over the centuries. The priest offers the sacrifice on behalf of the congregation. Because the representation of Calvary is something spiritual and invisible, the sacramental sacrifice tends to be identified with the words of the priest and his actions at the altar; and because the priest himself is quite unworthy to make this offering, so there has been a tendency to think of the priest as representing Christ when he makes the eucharistic offering. In this sense the priest is '*alter Christus*', a '*second Christ*'; and it is in this sense inappropriate for a woman to act the part of

Christ. But this is a secondary and degraded doctrine of the eucharistic sacrifice. There is no sense in which the priest himself offers the sacrifice: he is the officiant at the sacrificial representation in the bread and the wine of the one perfect sacrifice which Christ made once for all on Calvary. It therefore follows from a true view of eucharistic sacrifice that anyone who is the duly authorized representative of the church may be authorized to officiate.

Bishop Baker does not merely set forward this view of the eucharist on his own. On the contrary, he cites from Roman Catholic documents to show that this is the duly authorized eucharistic sacrifice which was defined at the Council of Trent[17] and confirmed at the Second Vatican Council[18] and set out in Pope Paul VI's encyclical *Mysterium Fidei*.[19] The Declaration of the Sacred Congregation of the Faith, in its attempt to provide theological reasons against the ordination of women, seems to put forward a corrupt mediaeval form of the eucharistic sacrifice, rather than that which is set out in the schemata of Vatican II. It is significant that the official commentary on the Declaration quotes, in favour of its doctrine that the priest is 'in persona Christi', a saying of St Thomas Aquinas in the Middle Ages, to the effect that 'the priest enacts the image of Christ, in whose person and by whose power he pronounces the words of consecration'.[20] The commentary continues: 'Although St Thomas gave us the reason for excluding women the much discussed one of the state of subjection ("status subjectionis"), he nevertheless took as his starting point the principle that "sacramental signs represent what they signify by a natural resemblance",[21] in other words the need for a "natural resemblance" between Christ and the person who is his sign.'[22] The commentary concludes (but without much argument) that 'it would not accord with "natural resemblance", with that obvious "meaningfulness", if the memorial of the Supper were to be carried out by a woman'. The Declaration seems to understand natural resemblance as referring not to the species *homo sapiens*, a person made in God's image, but only to a person of the male gender; yet it does not point out the differentiating characteristics of the male gender which make it imperative (in the view of the Sacred Congregation) that the President of the eucharist should be of the male sex.

Such matters are not discussed in the ARCIC Statements. Indeed in 1973, when the Canterbury Statement on Ministry and Ordination was produced, the question of women's ordination was only just assuming prime importance. But by the time that the Salisbury

Elucidation on that Statement was published in 1979, the question of women's ordination to the priesthood had become a matter of considerable general interest and ecumenical importance. In the Elucidation a paragraph is given over to this subject:

> Since the publication of the Statement (on *Ministry and Ordination*) there have been rapid developments with regard to the ordination of women. In those churches of the Anglican Communion where canonical ordinations of women have taken place, the bishops concerned believe that their action implies no departure from the traditional doctrine of the ordained ministry (as expounded for example in the Statement). While the Commission realizes that the ordination of women has created for the Roman Catholic Church a new and grave obstacle to the reconciliation of our communions (cf. Letter of Pope Paul VI to Archbishop Donald Coggan, 23 March 1976), it believes that the principles on which its doctrinal agreement rests are not affected by such ordinations; for it was concerned with the origin and nature of the ordained ministry and not with the question who can or cannot be ordained.[23]

A year earlier there had been published the Report of the Anglican-Roman Catholic Consultation on the Ordination of Women to the Priesthood. The difficulty experienced in authorization for its publication gives some indication of the negative feelings then current in Rome. It was agreed that the authority of the findings of the Consultation would be only that of its members.

The report of the Consultation is very non-committal. It does little more than clear the air, clarifying the situation both among Roman Catholics and among Anglicans and calling both for renewed mutual trust between the two Communions, and for a continuance of the dialogue which has been so fruitful among the members of ARCIC. Indeed, it called for a 'deeper dialogue on those noticeable differences which have been emphasized by this new obstacle – matters such as human sexuality, culture and tradition, freedom and authority, among others'. The report concluded:

> The rapidity of change in our times, the great diversities of culture and circumstances in which the churches must minister, and the growing characteristic contribution of the Third World to

theology demands openness, flexibility and a readiness to accept differences in form and style. How this is to be achieved in fidelity to the tradition which we share is one of the challenges which face the Church in our time.[24]

The Consultation noted two grounds for hope. The first was that the Anglican churches which have proceeded to ordain women to the presbyterate have done so in the conviction that they have not departed from traditional understanding of the apostolic ministry. And the second was that the Declaration does not explicitly affirm that the exclusion of women from the priesthood is *de jure divino*. In other words, it has not been authoritatively stated that the requirement by the Roman Catholic Church to ordain men only to the priesthood is made on divine authority in accordance with divine law. It is therefore capable of being altered, at least in principle. For all the excellent theological arguments that the Declaration (in the opinion of its authors) may have put forward in favour of the *status quo*, the door has not been finally shut on the admission of women to the presbyterate. The door may be closed, but it is not locked and barred. And the power of the keys (in this respect) rests with the Roman Catholic Church, for as the Declaration itself states: 'In the final analysis it is the Church through the voice of her magisterium, that, in these various domains decides what can change and what can remain immutable.'[25] Although the same Declaration states that 'the practice of the Church has a normative character', this does not absolutely preclude the possibility of change. It must be admitted however that, under Pope John Paul II the prospect of change in this matter is, humanly speaking, minimal. Indeed it is well known that there has been private correspondence between the Pope and Dr Robert Runcie, the Archbishop of Canterbury, on the 'grave obstacle' that the admission of women to the priesthood by Anglican Churches has put in the way of reunion between the two communions. Meanwhile, in the Anglican Communion, the movement for the ordination of women, far from receding, grows in strength. There are, at the time of writing, 741 women validly ordained to the presbyterate in the Anglican Communion. In the Episcopal Church of the USA some seminaries have as many women as men among their ordinands. Within that church the first soundings towards raising a women to the episcopate have been taken. Within the Anglican Communion as a whole, women have now been ordained (or ecclesiastical authority has been given for their ordination) in the Church of Hong Kong, the Episcopal Church of USA, Canada, New Zealand, Uganda, Kenya and Brazil. (Australia failed by two votes only.)

The chance of agreement between the Roman Catholic and the Anglican Churches on the subject of women's ordination does not seem great. It is often said that for the Church of England to go further down the road on which it has already embarked would make the situation more difficult. This may be marginally true, but already the Anglican Communion has begun to go this way, and the Roman Catholic Church is not having conversations just with the Church of England but with representatives of the whole Anglican Communion. The movement for the ordination of women within the Anglican Communion is far too widespread for it to be disregarded as a kind of minor Anglican anomaly (comparable perhaps to the anomalies that take place in most Local Ecumenical Projects, where there is a united congregation meeting in a single church building). On the contrary, the Lambeth Conference in 1978 recognized the fact that some constituent churches ordain women, and that account has to be taken of the actual realities of the situation. The eyes of many members of the Church of England seem closed to these realities of the Anglican Communion as a whole because, instinctively and perhaps subconsciously, they seem to assume that the Church of England comprises the only church of the Anglican Communion which has real importance. Certainly the Church of England is the mother church; but children grow up and supplant their mothers in numbers and vigour, if not in respect due to age.

Is there any way forward in this difficult situation? It is out of the question that those churches which presently ordain women to the presbyterate should cease to do so. It is not altogether impossible that the Roman Catholic Church should at some time ordain women as priests, but the contingency seems very remote in the more immediate future (even though this would solve that church's growing shortage of priests). If there is to be any understanding between the two churches, it must be on the basis of their present differences and actual situation.

So long as the ordination of women to the priesthood is not regarded as *de jure divino* in the Roman Catholic Church, some accommodation is possible. Each church could retain its own disciplines and rules, and its own reasons for so doing, together with basic agreements, such as we have already noted in the Canterbury Agreed Statement on Ministry and Ordination. If *Apostolicae Curae* is superseded, and if a way is found by the Roman Catholic Church to recognize Anglican orders, it is not to be expected that Anglican women's priestly orders would be recognized in that church unless and until they are recognized in the Roman Catholic Church as well. Neither church would condemn the other: each would continue in its own traditions; and care and courtesy would be shown to avoid hurting the scruples of the other. Priests of the Western catholic church have to be celibate, but they recognize the tradition of married priests in uniate churches, or (in some rare cases) the possibility of Anglican priests who were married before they became Roman Catholic being ordained within it as married men. The different traditions of celibacy and marriage in no way impair the recognition of Holy orders in these different traditions. In the same kind of way Roman Catholics could conceivably recognize male Anglican priests as belonging to another tradition. But they would not recognize Anglican women who have been ordained to the presbyterate since (so far) they have not themselves ordained women to this Holy order. Of course if such ordination were regarded as a travesty of what God wills, or as contrary to his intention, then a church which ordains women might be regarded as having distorted the catholic faith. But if it is recognized that such churches believe that they are maintaining the ancient catholic order of the church in an extended form, and if this is not authoritatively condemned as a heresy but regarded as a variant discipline, which does not distort or destroy the essentials of catholic order, then some kind of accommodation along the lines indicated above is clearly possible – unless there is fear that the ways of one church will infect and influence unduly the ways of the other. This however seems very improbable. The Roman Catholic Church may surely be assumed to be sufficiently sure of its own position not to fear too close a relationship to the different stance of another communion. Indeed, if that were the case, there would be little chance of a convergence between the two communions. But we have already noted as beyond doubt that the Holy Spirit is bringing the two communions closer together in faith and hope and love, in mutual friendship, understanding, and spirituality.

9

The Limits of Pluralism

After this brief survey of the major fields of difference between the Roman Catholic Church and the Churches of the Anglican Communion, it is appropriate to consider on a broader front the prospects of reunion. When differences are examined, it is easy to forget the agreements. In fact, Roman Catholics and Anglicans agree about far more than they differ. Furthermore, there has taken place what I have described earlier as the 'miracle of convergence'. Those who believe in the guidance of the Holy Spirit can hardly doubt that he is bringing these two Communions closer to each other in so many different ways. This forms one particular aspect of what is loosely called 'the Ecumenical Movement'.

It is important to analyse this movement. It is diffused generally throughout all the churches, and it shows itself in many different forms and in many different ways. Ecumenism is not a message that has been passed by hierarchical authority at the centre to the grass roots on the periphery. Nor has it been passed down from a series of church centres to the laity on the periphery. Donald Schon, in his book *Beyond the Stable State* (the essence of which is to be found in his 1970 Reith Lectures) describes these two similar models for the dissemination of innovation as 'classic nineteenth century models', and he contrasts them with a more modern model derived from the 'constellation firm'. 'Theories of diffusion have characteristically lagged behind the reality of emerging systems', he wrote. 'Prevailing models of directed diffusion still rest on the great social

inventions of the late nineteenth and early twentieth centuries . . .
These models of directed diffusion do not adequately describe the
diffusion systems from which they are derived . . . Even in their
reality, moreover, these great nineteenth-century proliferation-
of-centres systems were inherently limited. They suffered from
dependence on limited resources and competence at the primary
centre, from the rigidity of central doctrine, and from a feedback
loop within which information moved primarily between secondary
and primary centres.'[1] (By this he meant that information never
really reached people on the periphery.)

Schon instances the Human Rights movement in the USA to
illustrate his more modern model, but the Ecumenical Movement
among the churches provides another excellent illustration. For the
Ecumenical Movement is not a single movement which has arisen
hierarchically from the centre, or from a proliferation of centres,
and spread thence to the periphery of the church. On the contrary,
it has arisen through a variety of movements which have their origin
on the periphery (i.e. at the grass roots of the churches) and it has
spread throughout Christendom, even 'infecting' centres of power
and authority. Schon analyses certain features in his 'constellation'
model of diffusion.[2] There is no established centre. There is no
stable, centrally established message. The system of the movement
cannot be described as the diffusion of an established message from
a centre to a periphery. Its behaviour and international scope
depends on the infrastructure technology which permits rapid
communication.

Is this the right model by which to describe the provenance of the
Ecumenical Movement? Certainly its message is vague, it has no
established centre, and it arises as much from the periphery as the
centre. It is perhaps not surprising that it has bypassed to a large
extent, and has left relatively unaffected, the formal structures of
the institutional churches. For these are essentially hierarchical,
whether they be episcopal, presbyterian or congregational; and
there are few points of contact between a 'constellation' model of
innovation and the hierarchical structure of institutional churches.
This is particularly true of the Roman Catholic Church, whose
magisterium is more structured, and whose pyramidical hierarchy,
with its apex at the Bishop of Rome, is more pronounced than that
of any other church. This might account for the fact that the Roman
Catholic Church has embraced ecumenism with fervour in its most

recent foundation documents (e.g. in the Schemata of the Second Vatican Council), and yet it has been able to make least progress in integrating its structures with those of other churches.

When considering the prospect of reunion, it is with formal structures that we must be concerned. And here it must be said that, if there must be agreement on all basic matters of faith and morals before re-union is possible, then – humanly speaking – unity seems, if not a hopeless proposition, at least to be located where the rainbow ends. For despite the very large areas of agreement, there are grave difficulties still to be overcome before full agreement on faith and doctrine is possible between the Roman Catholic Church and the Churches of the Anglican Communion. It is sometimes said that the Anglican movement for the ordination of women to the ministerial priesthood of the church is a particularly grave obstacle to reunion. Even if this is the case, it seems a comparatively small matter besides doctrinal differences over the sources of the church's authority or its structures, to say nothing of Mariology and the role of the laity. There are large differences too in approach over matters of ethics, and especially sexual ethics. These have not yet been tackled by ARCIC. God can solve problems which seem impossible to human beings; but it is hard to see, humanly speaking, how these two differing traditions could converge to the point where substantial agreement is possible over all these matters.

A broad survey shows that many – although not all – differences focus on matters of sex. This does not merely apply to the ordination of women. It applies to doctrines concerning the Mother of God Incarnate. It applies also to questions concerning social ethics, and in particular sexual ethics. If the magisterium of the Roman Catholic Church is exclusively male and celibate, it is perhaps not surprising that there are differences on matters of faith and morals between that church and the churches of the Anglican Communion, where members of the magisterium may marry at their own discretion. Perhaps this too accounts for differences in attitude to the laity, since a married priest or bishop is in an intimate relationship with a lay person – his wife – and so he may be thought to be able to appreciate better the rights and role of lay persons. (I realize that I am writing this from an Anglican point of view, and the matter must look very different from a Roman Catholic point of view, where it might be said that the Anglican hierarchy, by virtue of its married clergy, may have a less detached and objective view of such matters on account of family involvement.) It does seem to me likely that the doctrines of the two communions will not fully converge until their married discipline is the same. It is well known that the fundamental relationships of human beings greatly colour their ways of thinking, however objective these may seem.

Our Christian faith, however, compels us to believe that progress can be made towards the reconciliation of the two communions. In order to consider how this can be possible, it is necessary to examine models of unity.

It is commonly assumed that the goal is 'organic unity', although this concept is not always subjected to rigorous scrutiny. The word 'organic' presupposes an organism, a living being, made up of many parts and members, but functioning as one living unity, the quality of whose life is far greater than the sum of its parts. An organism is an organized body with connected interdependent parts sharing a common life. This model is derived from the Pauline doctrine of the church as the body of Christ. However, when Pauline usage is examined, the word 'body' is employed here with a variety of meanings and in different contexts.[3] Sometimes it refers to a particular church, and sometimes to the whole church of God. It is an open question whether it is intended to be understood ontologic-ally or merely analogically.[4] If the latter, it becomes just one of many images used to describe the church, such as bride, temple, etc.

The Vatican II *Dogmatic Constitution on the Church* prefers the phrases 'pilgrim church' or 'the People of God' to that of the Body of Christ, although it uses the latter. Where does the unity of the church lie in Roman Catholic teaching?

> Individual bishops are the visible fundamental principle of unity in their churches. These churches are moulded to the likeness of the universal Church; in them and of them consists the one, sole Catholic Church. For this reason individual bishops represent their own church; all, together with the Pope, represent the whole Church linked by peace, love and unity.[5]

It is unity with the Pope that for Roman Catholics guarantees the unity of the whole church: nonetheless the whole Catholic Church is present within a diocese, provided its bishop is in unity with the Roman Pontiff. Structurally speaking this seems a complex form of organic unity, if the whole Catholic Church can in some sense be present within a single diocese. It is rather like the human body, in so far as it consists of interdependent parts, while each of its billions of cells contains the genetic code of the whole body. It is a complex kind of organic unity.

The Roman Catholic Church contains within its organic unity Uniate Churches with their own discipline, liturgical practice, and theological and spiritual heritage. Some of these are the ancient patriarchates, which have given birth to daughter churches. The *Dogmatic Constitution on the Church* speaks of them thus: 'This agreement in diversity on the part of local churches is a brighter demonstration of the catholicity of the undivided Church.'[6] However these Uniate Churches do not differ from the rest of the church so far as faith and morals are concerned, and they acknowledge the Bishop of Rome as the supreme Primate of the church, with the same rights and status as the rest of the Roman Catholic Church accords him. So long as differences in faith and morals still exist between the Roman Catholic Church and the churches of the Anglican Communion, Uniate Churches do not provide an adequate model whereby these Anglican churches can be related to the Roman Catholic Church.

Is a further degree of diversity possible than that of Uniate Churches? When I was Vicar of Great St Mary's, in 1970, I invited Cardinal Jan Willebrandts to come over from the Vatican Secretariat for Promoting Christian Unity (of which he was then President) to preach from the pulpit of that church. His sermon of 18 January 1970 (at the beginning of the Octave of Prayer for Christian Unity) was a notable occasion, but his words did not gain the wider hearing that they deserved.[7] He began by quoting from Piers Plowman:

. . . come with me you fools,
Into unity of Holy Church – and hold we us there . . .
And call we to all the commons – that they come into Unity
And there abide and do battle – against Belial's children.

Willebrandts went on to speak of the hierarchy of truth and to quote the words of John XXIII: 'One thing is the deposit of faith, that is the truths preserved within our sacred doctrine, another is the way they are expressed while retaining the same meaning and substance.' He then developed his main thesis:

May I invite you to reflect on a notion which, it seems to me, has received much fruitful attention from theologians recently? It is that of the *typos* in its sense of general form or character, and of a plurality of *typoi* within the communion of the one and only Church of Christ.

Cardinal Willebrandts made it clear that he was not referring to the local and particular church.

> The notion which I submit to your attention, that of a *typos* of a church, does not primarily designate a diocese or a national church (although in some cases it may more or less coincide with a national church). It is a nation which has its own phenomenological aspects, with their particular meaning.

The Cardinal went on to quote from the Vatican *Decree on Ecumenism*: 'For many centuries the Churches of East and West went their own ways, though a brotherly communion of faith and sacramental life bound them together.'[8] He commented on this statement in a way that was fresh and important:

> The theological element which must always be present and presupposed is the full 'communion of faith and sacramental life'. But the words 'went their own ways' point in the direction of the notion which I would like to develop a little more. What are these 'own ways' and when can we speak of a *typos*? A bit further on, the *Decree on Ecumenism* explains: 'the heritage handed down by the apostles was received in different forms and ways, so that from the very beginnings of the Church it has had a varied development in various places thanks to a similar variety of natural gifts and conditions of life.'

The Cardinal then addressed himself to the situation in England where the Roman Catholic Church and the Church of England exist side by side. He went on to say:

> Different *typoi* exist in countries where eastern and western Churches live together. If within one nation two *typoi* are so closely related, that in a situation of close communion between then, Providence draws them into coalescence, the authentic and strong elements of each will take their place in an enriched unity. Such a strengthening and enrichment will manifest itself primarily where it finds its highest motive – in a renewal of witness to Christ, a renewal of mission.

Cardinal Willebrandts prudently did not elaborate on whether he had in mind something more than existing Uniate Churches. When he spoke of a 'full communion of faith and sacramental life', he would seem to have drawn a distinction, at least implicit, between faith and its articulated exposition in terms of doctrine. And this distinction is very important.

Hans Küng is no longer regarded as a 'teacher of the Roman Catholic Church' but he was so regarded when he wrote *The Church*; and his words there about doctrine are important. He wrote:

> Every formulation of faith, whether made by an individual or by the whole Church, remains imperfect, incomplete, unclear, partial and fragmentary.[9]

Because truth involves a personal apprehension of reality rather than mere assent to propositions, all dogmas have an inbuilt unsatisfactoriness.[10] Küng was particularly concerned with the distinction between truth and error. He went on in the passage quote above:

> Any human statement of truth, because of its human limitations, is very close to error and one has only to overlook the human limitations of truth to turn truth into error. All human truth stands in the shadow of error. All error contains at least a grain of truth. What a true statement says is true; what it fails to say may also be true. It is a simplified view of truth to suppose that every sentence in its verbal formulation must be either true or false. On the contrary any sentence can be true *and* false, according to its purpose, its context, its underlying meaning. It is much harder to discover what is meant by it than what it says. A sincere, fearless and critical ecumenical theology must give up throwing dogmas at the head of the other side.

That is precisely what the Second Vatican Council achieved. No longer were we given Decrees complete with anathemas: on the contrary, we had Dogmatic Constitutions pastorally oriented and non-polemically and uncontroversially worded. These Constitutions may be contrasted with what Küng, in *The Structures of the Church*, called 'polemic orientation' of dogma. 'Herein lies the great task of theology and of the Church', he wrote, 'namely, to rediscover the inner balance of faith and to lead it back to its original organic unity of tensions.'[11]

It is here that progress would seem to lie. The Anglican

Communion has produced a different *typos* from that of the Western Catholic Church. If we look for example at the Mariological dogmas of the Roman Catholic Church and ask ourselves what underlies these dogmatic statements, we can find truths about the humanity of Christ and about his divinity which are expressed otherwise in Anglican theology. Or again we can find the development of one *typos*, in a church whose magisterium is exclusively male and celibate, that is rather different from another church whose *typos* has been moulded by a tradition of married priesthood. Both believe that they have authentic expressions of the same catholic faith; and while they recognize that the other has exactly the same convictions about its own expression of faith, both recognize that the articulated dogmatic expression of that common faith differs in ways that make it difficult for the one to accept the other's. But, once again, if we look at the polemical orientation of each other's dogmas, then it is more comprehensible how each has come in certain respects to diverge from the other.

Even if this position be granted, it will still be necessary to circumscribe the limits of pluralism within the one church. The Lambeth Fathers issued an Appeal to All Christian People in 1920 on the basis of the so called 'Lambeth Quadrilateral' of the One Bible, the common Creeds, the Gospel Sacraments, and the historic threefold Order of the Church. ARCIC has added to these the acceptance of a Universal Primate. Is there any way in which a Universal Primate could be accepted by both churches without loss of integrity on the part of either?

Here an analogy may be useful from a secular source. The British Commonwealth of Nations represents the largest voluntary grouping of nations that the world has ever seen. It consists of forty-nine sovereign independent states, and comprises just under one-fifth of the total land area of the globe, and one in four of its population. What is the formal sign of the unity of this vast voluntary grouping of mankind? It is the acknowledgment of the Sovereign of the United Kingdom of Great Britain and Northern Ireland as Head of the Commonwealth. The Queen is the bond of unity, the personal symbol of unity who provides a personal link between its billion plus members. And at the same time her function is not the same throughout the Commonwealth. As Queen of England she has some particular functions, and all government is carried out in her name. She is Queen too of other Commonwealth countries, with diminished functions, and infrequent visits. She is Head of the Commonwealth for other constituent countries which are Republics, with their own President and chief minister. Within this very disparate aggregation of people, she has different functions for different groups, although she is the one symbol of unity for all.

Here at least is a kind of analogy for a future re-united Christendom. If the church were to reunite on the basis of the five cardinal characteristics outlined above – an Ecumenical Pentagon rather than a Lambeth Quadrilateral – it would at least be conceivable that the Bishop of Rome, as Universal Primate, could have different functions for different groupings. For the Roman Catholic Church he would continue to have the same relationship as he does now, and similarly with the Uniate Churches which form part of the Roman Catholic Church. But it is at least conceivable that the Anglican Communion could recognize in him the Universal Primate of the Church, in the sense of the formal symbol of unity rather than the Vicar of Christ and the Roman Pontiff with 'full supreme and universal power over the whole Church'.[12] Under the grace and providence of God, churches (with a common ministerial priesthood, except that it would not be expected that women would be recognized as priests in other churches) could grow together into the 'coalescence' of which Cardinal Willebrandts spoke, where 'the authentic and strong elements of each will take their place in an enriched unity'.

It is clear that St Paul was in substantial but not complete agreement with St Peter, St James and St John in the visit recorded in the second chapter of the Epistle to the Galatians. The fact however that they were not in complete agreement did not prevent a mutual recognition of their different ministries between St Paul and St Barnabas on the one hand and St Peter, St James and St John on the other.

If a common ministerial priesthood were recognized between the Church of England and the Roman Catholic Church, does the concept of unity outlined above accord with the biblical doctrine of the 'one church', which should be normative for our efforts towards unity? Here attention may be drawn to St John's Gospel where Jesus prays:

It is not for these alone that I pray, but for those also who through their words put their faith in me; may they all be one: as thou, Father, art in me, and I in thee, so also may they be in us, that the world may believe that thou didst send me. The glory which thou gavest me I have given to them, that they may be one, as we are one; I in them and thou in me, may they be perfectly one (John 17.20–23a).

Earlier Jesus has said: 'I and the Father are one' (John 10.5). But the Greek text of that verse does not contain the masculine form of *heis*, but the neuter *hen*. Clearly there is not intended a metaphysical identity between the Father and the Son. Their unity is more complex and hidden in mystery. After all, *homoousios* is far more mysterious than Patripassianism. Since the unity of Christian believers is dependent upon the unity of the Father and the Son, it follows that the unity of the church is not a simple identity of all believers in an undifferentiated unity, but a deeper and more complex mystery, similar to that between the Father and the Son. For Jesus prays *hina pantes hen osi*, that they may all be 'one thing', or 'at one' or 'united', or however it is best translated. What the text does not mean is that 'they may all be one' which is how it is usually simplistically translated. Since the text refers both to the mutual coinherence of the Father and the Son, and the mutual coinherence of believers with the Father and the Son, clearly what is being prayed for is not a particular form of outward or even simple organic unity, but a spiritual unity of believers in God which may be expressed in the way which is best adapted to the circumstances of the church.

This suggestion about a future form of unity based on a secular model may or may not commend itself.[13] The argument of this book in no way depends upon it. What has been attempted here is to rejoice at the growing degree of convergence between the Roman Catholic Church and the Churches of the Anglican Communion, to note the amount of doctrinal agreement which is reflected in the Agreed Statements of the Anglican-Roman Catholic International Commission, and to attempt to point out, honestly and rigorously, the different stances, attitudes and dogmas of the two Communions in certain matters of faith and morals. This has been done in the conviction that it is only when these differences are clarified and understood that there arises a genuine possibility of mutual understanding and acceptance. I end with the heartfelt prayer that the Holy Spirit, in his own time, will guide and direct the People of God not only into the ways of holiness and catholicity and apostolicity, but also into that form of unity which is his will.

Appendix

In the chapter on 'Women and the Ministerial Priesthood' it was explained that the Church of England is divided on the subject of admission of women to the priesthood. In order to illustrate the divisions existing in the church, two speeches (one in favour by the author, and the other against by the Rt Revd Graham Leonard) which opened the debate in the General Synod on 8 November 1978 are reproduced here from *Report of Proceedings*, General Synod, vol. 9, no. 3 (November 1978), pp. 996–1011. Although some of the references are by now out of date (there are now many more women priests and further provinces of the Anglican Communion have decided to ordain women; and negotiations with the Free Churches have broken down), nonetheless the arguments used on both sides are still in general use.

The Bishop of Birmingham (Rt Revd H. W. Montefiore):

I beg to move:

'That this Synod asks the Standing Committee to prepare and bring forward legislation to remove the barriers to the ordination of women to the priesthood and their consecration to the episcopate.'

When Prof. Macquarrie opened the hearing on the ordination of women at the recent Lambeth Conference, he began with the words: 'I think I must have been out of my mind when I accepted the invitation to speak on this subject.' There is no need for me to say that, because many of you have thought that about me for years! But, like Prof. Macquarrie, I too should like to argue that this debate need not be and should not be explosive. One of the marked features of the Lambeth discussions was the mutual forbearance, charity and self-restraint on both sides, despite strongly-held convictions. Pray God today's debate will be the same. The eyes of the church, if not the eyes of the world, are upon us now; and we all need – I as much as you – the prime requisites of truth, openness and mutual forbearance throughout the whole of this debate.

First must come truth. I am convinced, along with the majority of the General Synod who voted in July 1975, that there are no fundamental objections to the ordination of women to the priest-hood. I believe this to be a matter of truth, and I dare not put quick reunion, or even the immediate welfare of the church, before the claims of truth. Of course a vote of General Synod does not make anything true, any more than the Council of Constantinople made the Nicene Creed true in AD 381. No, what Councils and Synods can do is to recognize truth; and I believe that our General Synod did this in 1975.

This debate is not intended to cover all that ground again. I am going to give only the briefest summary why that was the verdict. First, the Pontifical Biblical Commission is said to have concluded, the biblical evidence does not allow any final settlement of the question. Second, the fact that women never have been ordained to the presbyterate does not mean that they never can be. As the 1968 Lambeth Conference reported, the New Testament does not encourage Christians to think that nothing should be done for the first time. Tradition can grow and develop. Third, the ministerial priesthood is representative of God in Christ. But God himself is neither male nor female; and what matters about the Incarnation is that God assumed human nature. As the Greek fathers declared, the Word became *anthropos*, not *aner*. Since priesthood represents humanity to God and God to humanity, it is humanity and not maleness which is the decisive qualification for exercising priest-hood; just as in Christ, according to catholic doctrine, it is his humanity which is of saving significance, and not the accidents of that humanity.

For Prof. Macquarrie's purposes, it was enough that no decisive theological objections could be found. But not for mine. I must go further. I must show why the matter is so important that steps should be taken now to remove the barriers to women's ordination. As I have said, this is a matter of truth. It takes time and circumstances for truths implicit in the revolutionary gospel of Christ to be recognized – and no doubt there are further time-bombs hidden in Christian revelation, ticking away until the times are ripe. But once truth is perceived, we have a sacred duty to act upon it.

Now in times past women felt able to be fully represented by men. I need not labour how the status of women has changed. To insist on an all-male priesthood in a society which has abandoned all-male leadership in other areas of life is to distort the meaning of Christian priesthood. It leads to serious distortion in doctrine. If the priesthood is to be fully representative, if it is to be catholic in the real sense of the word, we need both men and women. If we do not extend the historic ministry of the church in response to these major changes in the ordering of our society, we endanger the church's mission to the world. I repeat, we endanger our mission to the world.

Next, I quote from the famous 1920 Lambeth Encyclical, with its Appeal to All Christian People. The bishops said this then about the ministry of women: 'Everywhere the attempt must be made to make room for the Spirit to work, according to the wisdom which he will give, so that the fellowship of the ministry may be strengthened by the co-operation of women, and the fellowship of the church enriched by their spiritual gifts.' We badly need in the ordained ministry today those special gifts and wisdom which women alone can bring to the priestly role.

Finally, we can actually perceive, if we have eyes to see, women priests at work. Already there are women priests working in the Anglican Communion. They exist. Their priestly ministry is welcomed. Speaking personally, I must confess that it was not until I was in Hong Kong and I saw a woman priest about her business that I realized that she was not a female priest any more than I am a male priest: we were both children of God called by him to the priesthood. Her ministry was as valid and authentic as mine. There are now, as members know, women ordained in Hong Kong, America, Canada, and New Zealand. There is a woman who is an archdeacon, a canon residentiary, one called to serve on a diocesan standing committee, the highest office we were told, strangely enough, open to a priest in that diocese. In America alone, up to April of this year, 113 women were priests and 143 deacons.

What is more, in our own country there are women who truly believe they are called by God to the priesthood. Not long ago a woman came to see me who is in a highly responsible position, who is widely respected for her Christian character. She told me of her inner call to the priesthood. By any criterion that I could apply to a male ordinand, her sense of vocation was authentic. What was I to tell her? Was I to tell her that it must be a delusion, because she has an X chromosome where I have a Y? Or was I to say: 'There is no fundamental objection to your ordination, but the church says, No?' That would seem to me to put the convenience of men before the call of God. Remember that almost a quarter of the women in full-time ministry in our church have said they would seek ordination to the priesthood, if it were possible. At the very earliest they could not be ordained for five years. Can this Synod put them off longer than that without even testing their vocation?

These are the four compelling reasons why we must go ahead now. At this point I must say a word about deacons and bishops. If this motion is carried today, as I hope it will be, there must also be consequential legislation to declare a deaconess not only in orders, but also in holy orders, as recommended by the 1968 Lambeth Conference. This is a complex area, and I am not going to be sidetracked into it now. But I must point it out.

As for bishops, I cannot imagine that a woman priest would be put forward by the Crown Appointments Commission for election to a see in the near future. No one knows better than myself that that body is capable of strange recommendations, but not that yet. At present, alas, a woman bishop might be not so much a focus of unity as a cause for disunity. The Lambeth bishops urged caution at this very point. But then I am not proposing that women should be made bishops yet. I am asking that the legal barriers be removed, which is quite another matter. To make it legally possible for women to be priests but not bishops would be real sexual discrimination. And while male headship is a permissible Anglican doctrine, it is not to be imposed on everyone as a necessary Anglican doctrine. The scriptures do not demand it. And if you look at our liturgy to discover our doctrine, you will find we have authorized two marriage services where the wife's vow of obedience is purely optional.

Let us consider in turn some objections against passing the motion before us.

First, 'Look at the churches where women are ordained, in Sweden and America.' Well, let us look at them. In Sweden women have been ordained for twenty years. Of course, there was State pressure there, but the Dean of Stockholm recently told me, ten days ago, that if women had not been ordained, the position in the church would be far more serious than it is today; and even today, the overwhelming majority of committed Christian lay people are in favour of it, not to say the majority of the clergy.

Then look at America – but do not pass judgment, because their culture is different from our own. They actually enjoy confrontation, and they tend to politicize where we play things down. In any case, Americans believe that they did make all proper consultations and that their voting procedure was fair; and they told us at Lambeth that the present schism is only partly about women's ordination, and that it is not of great significance; but if women had not been ordained, then there would have been a very grave schism indeed.

Second, 'We ought to wait for a General Council before taking such a step.' But how could we have a General Council of all Christians when the Orthodox have not even succeeded in having one of their own themselves? In any case, the church of God does not work by waiting for General Councils. Peter did not wait for the Council at Jerusalem before he baptized Cornelius. No, when he saw that God had poured out his Spirit on him, he went ahead and baptized him. The Council later ratified what he had done. That is the way God's work goes forward. The part paves the way for the whole. Anglicans who ordain women do so in the conviction that they are keeping to the historic ministry of the church – I would not want to suggest that we jettison that – and I believe that we will render all catholic Christendom a positive service by deciding to go ahead today.

Third, 'Ordaining women will destroy chances of reunion with Rome.' I just do not believe it. I know that Pope Paul VI spoke of this development as a 'grave and new obstacle to unity'. So it may be. But women priests are already a part – and an accepted part – of Anglicanism, and they are here to stay. I think it would be better if Roman Catholics took us as we are, rather than as some people think we ought to be. No decision taken at this Synod can alter the face that women priests are an accepted part of Anglicanism. In any case, ecumenism does not mean prevaricating over what you know is right, in case you upset other churches. It means doing what you know to be right, and trusting that other churches which think differently will accept you in love and truth. Pope John Paul II has already committed himself to ecumenism. Bishop Daly, speaking recently on behalf of the Secretariat for Christian Unity, naturally affirmed that the Vatican Declaration is not a temporary but a permanent position. How could he do otherwise? But consider what he did not say. He did not say that if we ordained women, it would prevent further growth into unity. He did not deny that the matter is a *quaestio disputata* – a disputed question – how could he, when so many well-known Roman Catholic theologians affirm they are unconvinced that women cannot be ordained?

In any case, the official report of the Anglican/Roman Catholic Consultation on the subject sees two grounds for hope: first, that Anglicans who ordain women to the priesthood believe that they have not departed from the traditional understanding of the apostolic ministry – this is also written into the Lambeth Resolution – and second, that the Roman Catholic Declaration does not say the matter is *de jure divino* – of divine law. Further – and this is important – there is nothing in the ARCIC Agreed Statement on Ministry which is opposed to the ordination of women. While Rome can never of course withdraw past declarations, it is conceivable that a development in her doctrine of priesthood could bypass this as well as other problems. It has done this kind of thing in the past.

Fourth, 'Ordaining women will jeopardize our special relationship with the Orthodox.' Well, this is something we must face. We hope it will not. It would be tragic if our progress towards unity should be halted now, after so long a special relationship, stretching right back to Archbishop Theodore of Tarsus. But I cannot believe this will happen. Firstly, we are not asking the Orthodox to ordain women: we ask them to accept the good faith of Anglicans who see this as an extension of the historic apostolic ministry. We do not judge them, for example, over the exclusion from Mount Athos of women – or indeed even hens! We simply accept that they are different from us. I see here two grounds for hope. First, serious dialogue with the Orthodox on this matter is only just beginning; and second, at this very time (this is not generally known) the Orthodox have just agreed to set up ecclesial conversations with the Lutheran World Federation, and some of those churches have ordained women for twenty-five years. What is possible for Lutherans is possible for Anglicans too.

Fifth, 'It will end the Bonn Agreement with the Old Catholics.' Oh no, it will not. It is true that Old Catholics do not ordain women and will no longer take part in our consecrations. But they are still in full communion with us. The only exception is the Polish National Catholic Church in the USA. Their Prime Bishop took unilateral action against the advice of the Old Catholics International Bishops Conference. The Old Catholics as a whole have not broken with us, and do not intend to do so.

Sixth, 'It will damage the ecumenical movement.' In the old days people used to say that ecumenism was really pan-Protestantism in disguise. Nowadays you might wonder whether it is non pan-Catholicism in disguise. We must not forget that most Protestant Churches ordain women as ministers. We have a record of closer relations with the Free Churches in this country than with the Roman Catholics. For example, the Roman Catholics regard our male orders, the orders of every Anglican priest in this Synod, as 'absolutely null and utterly void'; but the Free Churches do not. We have agreed in this Synod to prepare a covenant with Free Churches which already ordain women. In our vote at the last Group of Sessions, we agreed then not to raise the question of women's ordination. But the question will not go away. I was in touch with the Executive Officer of the Churches Unity Commission just before he retired, and he authorized me to say the following: 'Mutual recognition must include all ministers. It would be unthinkable for the Free Churches to be asked to ditch their women ministers.' Conceivably there might be an understanding that the Church of England, although it recognizes those women ministers, would not avail itself of their services. This would be a fantastic position, to recognize their women ministers and to refuse to ordain women ourselves.

Eighth, 'We need more time.' People always say that. Just consider. Women's ministry came to the forefront when the Bishop of London 115 years ago – I am not referring to the present Bishop of London – ordained a deaconess. Half a century ago Charles Raven wrote a pamphlet on the ordination of women. I sat at his feet when he lectured on the subject in Cambridge in the 1950s. The present debate was sparked off by a report sixteen years ago. The accusation of 'instant theology' just does not hold. What is more, it will take five years before a final vote, needing a two-thirds majority, can be taken in this Synod. During that time dialogue will continue – for example, John Ritches recently wrote a paper for the Orthodox Conversations which he hopes to publish in the spring with comments by Dr Eric Mascall. We must let due process continue without any special pause. Do not forget that the Lambeth bishops overwhelmingly rejected an amendment which called for such a pause, pending an evaluation by the Anglican Primates. (Incidentally, one of the better notices given out at the Lambeth Conference requested the all Primates Committee to meet in Darwin College!)

Ninth, 'It will break up the Anglican Communion.' On the

contrary, the Anglican Communion emerged from the Lambeth Conference with a new confidence and a new sense of identity. It differs from the Protestant Churches by its insistence on the historic apostolic ministry. It differs from the Roman and Orthodox Churches – and here I quote from the Lambeth Resolution – because 'the holding together of diversity within a unity of faith and worship is part of the Anglican heritage'. There is no question of the break-up of the Anglican family. The children have grown up, and as in any family there are sometimes disagreements. Some go one way, some another. But the family is determined to stay together, and anyone who thinks otherwise is utterly mistaken.

Tenth, 'If we ordain women we shall tear apart the Church of England.' If we did so now, then that might be true. But if we continue with all due process, it will not be true. It was not so in Canada or New Zealand or Hong Kong; and in the USA the schism is miniscule. In any case the motion before us is not that we ordain women now but that we prepare legislation to remove the legal barriers to ordination and consecration of women. That is very, very different. I have here a timetable which informs us that the very earliest we can have a Final Approval motion needing a two-thirds majority is July 1983, and if you were particularly obstructive it might not be until February 1985. Today's decision will only be part of a long process.

I, for one, will not consent to the alienation of my dear friends in Christ who do not agree with me in this matter. I value the unity of our church – and its historic ministry – as much as anyone in this Synod. Precisely because we are talking about an extension of the historic ministry, I believe that Catholics can vote in favour. But although my four positive reasons for going ahead are compelling for me, and although my demolition of the ten objections is equally decisive, I recognize that this may not, alas, be the case for everyone. It may not be the case for the Bishop of Truro. We must respect one another. We must allow a pluralism of practice. It happened in the early church. Just imagine a church which could accept James the Lord's brother as its leader, who kept all the 613 precepts of the Jewish law, and also Paul, who claimed to be all things to all men. Think, too, of the difference of practice – and I think very often of this as a Jew – between Jews and Gentiles in the early church, and the forbearance that was shown on both sides. My dear friends, we must show forbearance, we must respect each other, we must allow similar diversity. There is hierarchy of truth, and no one can claim that the ordination of women is at the top.

Our Anglican comprehensiveness is based on sound theology, and we find this spelled out in the New Testament. I remind you of the forbearance of Paul in Romans 14, which is relevant today: 'You, sir, why do you pass judgment on your brother? And you, sir, why do you hold your brother in contempt?' Whatever decision we take on this matter, we cannot avoid conflict. We shall find a way through. With love and forbearance we can find a way through, and I believe that Anglicanism has a special contribution to make as a pontifical church, holding within itself, as it has always done, differing views about ministry. What we must do is to allow ourselves liberty of action and freedom of conscience, so that those who, alas, do not accept women priests do not act against their conscience – any legislation must contain a conscience clause with adequate safeguards, and if need be compensation. In any case, the Benefices Measure will ensure that no parish has a women priest as incumbent if that is not acceptable.

But if one side enjoys liberty in Christ Jesus, so too must the other. If the majority want women to be ordained, let due process go steadily on, until we see when it comes to the final vote what we cannot see now, whether or not there is an adequate consensus to go forward. Remember that in a recent enquiry conducted by National Opinion Polls, over two-thirds of those questioned – yes, even two-thirds of those who said they were weekly Anglican churchgoers – approved of the ordination of women.

Remember that, among your fathers-in-God, no single bishop of the Church of England voted at Lambeth against a Resolution which recognized women priests as acceptable within the Anglican Communion, and I could see only three who abstained – Peterborough, Chichester and Hereford.

All the statistics suggest that there is a growing consensus about the ordination of women. I do not know when it will reach acceptable proportions. But, my brothers and sisters in Christ, do not, I beg of you, do not quench the Holy Spirit of God. Do not shut the door now. Remember Gamaliel – if this be of God, it will prosper. Only vote against us if you believe women are incapable of receiving the grace of orders. Vote for us, as I hope you will, if you agree with us; and if you cannot, then I beg you to be forbearing and to give us our liberty and abstain. Give us our liberty of action in

Christ Jesus as you will have yours. Above all, let God call whom he
wills, not whom we will, to the priestly ministry of the Church.

The Bishop of Truro (Rt Revd Graham Leonard):

At the end of my speech I shall appeal for the same forbearance and
charity in this debate to which the Bishop of Birmingham has
referred, but before I begin I should like to endorse what he said
about the way in which this matter should be considered by us as a
Christian body.

Shortly before the Lambeth Conference in July, a book was
published by Prof. Stephen Sykes, the Van Mildert Professor of
Divinity in the University of Durham. It was entitled *The Integrity
of Anglicanism*, and that is the real substance of our debate today. It
is for this reason that many of us are so deeply concerned about the
outcome. It is for this reason that we cannot accept that the
ordination of women is a matter of secondary importance. It raises
some of the central issues of the Christian faith and the principles
which give the Church of England its identity.

This concern is felt by those who are unable to accept the
ordination of women to the priesthood on theological grounds. It is
shared by those who believe there are no theological objections but
judge that, in the words of the Revd Peter Cornwell in *The Times*, this
issue is too big for such a small section of Christians as the Anglican
Communion to decide by itself. 'There are certain things', he wrote,
'which Anglicans are capable of deciding on . . . But there are
certain things which we hold in common with other Christians, such
as the Creeds and the Canon of scripture. Experience shows that if
you tamper unilaterally with these bands of unity you cause Christian
disunity. Because Anglicans have claimed that the ministry lies in this
category of "common property" any substantial change in its
ordering must depend on the decision of the common body. This is
just as much a matter of principle and conscience as any which the
advocates of women priests may invoke.' To his words I would add
that a change in the historic ministry is of particular significance in
that it changes what is done rather than what is thought. The historic
ministry is part of the framework maintained by the Church of
England which has given it freedom of interpretation. When the
framework is changed that freedom is imperilled.

Mr Cornwell's words reflect the traditional claim of Anglicans so
clearly expressed by Archbishop Geoffrey Fisher, 'We have no

doctrine of our own – we only possess the catholic doctrine of the Catholic Church.'

Bishop Wand wrote, 'If its organization is the most obvious feature of any church, the most important must assuredly be its faith.' We must ask, 'By what criteria is the continued expression of the faith of the Church of England in a changing world to be tested if it is to retain its integrity?' We must then apply these criteria to any changes or developments which are proposed and try to discern whether they be of God or whether they spring from our conformity to the world. It is the evident lack of this discernment which troubles many devoted intelligent lay people such as the Member of Parliament who wrote to me a short while ago asking why the Church of England appeared to accept the criteria of secular thought so readily and failed to emphasize the eternal truths which give true stability and challenge the assumptions of the world. The fact that the Church of England claims to be both catholic and reformed lays it open to special temptations in its relation to other churches – temptations to speak from its catholic element when speaking to churches in the catholic tradition and from its reformed element when speaking to the reformed churches. The Church of England has, as Bishop Stephen Neill has pointed out, a most honourable record in the ecumenical movement. It has earned that record when it has been true to itself and resisted these temptations.

So we must look at our title deeds and at the way in which Anglicans have sought to test the expression of our faith in successive generations. Before we do so, I must refer to the Resolutions of the Lambeth Conference on the ordination of women to the priesthood and to the episcopate – Resolutions 21 and 22.

We must recognize quite frankly and openly that the Lambeth Conference did not solve the problem. What it did was to buy time to enable the matter to be considered at the theological depth which is necessary. It did so in a spirit of charity – of that those who were present were very conscious indeed. It recognized that the Anglican Communion is deeply divided on the matter. It respects the legal autonomy of member churches. It asks us all to accept that this is so, to respect each other's convictions – and the report itself recognizes that there are theological convictions – and not to make matters worse while further consideration is given to the wider context of the theology of ministry and priesthood both amongst ourselves and

ecumenically. Of the need for such further consideration there is
not the slightest doubt.

We must now pass to the questions, 'What is the faith of
Anglicanism?' and 'By what criteria does it discern developments?'
It has always been the claim of the Anglican Church that in faith and
order it is in continuous identity with the primitive church. Dr
McAdoo, Archbishop of Dublin and co-Chairman of ARCIC – and
surely a sort of archetypal Anglican if ever there were one – says
that our commitment to the faith once for all delivered to the saints
is 'formative for the Anglican ethos and it means that the content of
faith cannot be changed by addition or omission'. He goes on to
point out that tradition is not a second source of revelation (which I
might add seems to me to be the view of some of the proponents, as
if the church in the second half of the twentieth century could be
given a new revelation not vouchsafed to earlier generations).
Tradition is, and again I quote, 'the experience of the Church living
and proclaiming that by which it lives and the test and criteria of the
continuous experience is scripture. The Anglican Church then
acknowledges tradition but tradition controlled by scripture.'

His words echo those written some forty years earlier by that
great biblical scholar, Sir Edwyn Hoskyns: 'The Gospel of the
church is grounded in a particular history since it is grounded in the
life and death of Jesus of Nazareth in Palestine at a particular epoch.
The peculiar claim of the Church is that this particular history is of
universal and ultimate significance. This note is sounded clearly and
concisely by each New Testament author and their chief concern is
to prevent the church from losing this Palestinian historical control.'
'It was the work of the Apostles', he continues, 'to preserve the
church from a conception of the work of the Spirit distinct from and
independent of the work of Jesus.' In other words, the Anglican
Church is committed to both a vertical and a horizontal control as it
seeks to live, proclaim and be faithful to the gospel, a vertical
obedience to God in the Spirit and a horizontal obedience to God in
Christ, of which scripture is the effective and determinative
instrument. The right course is known by giving each element an
equal degree of control. It is this lashing of the eternal gospel to its
historical moorings which must rule out for Anglicans that attitude
to divine revelation which is described as 'developmental theology'.
By that term I mean the view that secular thought at any one point in
history can justify theological changes which are not implicit in the

revelation contained in scripture and agreeable to the same.

So Bishop Michael Ramsey could write of the post-Apostolic church: 'Developments then took place but they were all tested. The tests of a true development are whether it bears witness to the Gospel, whether it expresses the general consciousness of Christians, and whether it serves the organic unity of the church in all its parts. These tests are summed up in the scriptures wherein the historical gospel and the experience of the redeemed and the nature of the Body are described. Hence while the Canon of scripture is itself a development, it has a special authority to control and check the whole field of development in life and doctrine.'

It is by these tests that we must assess the admitted innovation, or, strictly speaking, the revival of an innovation, for as far back as the early third century Irenaeus condemned Marcion both for his cavalier treatment of scripture and his attempts to ordain women, and we must begin with scripture. It is when I read the treatment of scripture by the proponents that I am most deeply disturbed, for in order to maintain that the proposal is consonant with scripture they seem to me to have to eviscerate it of almost all authority. Those advocates whose writings I have read – and I have tried to read as many as possible – seem to have to admit that scripture taken at its face value does not support them and to have to explain it away in various manners.

This does not surprise me, for while it is unthinkable to attribute gender to God – and I must repeat that as strongly as I can, because it is frankly a travesty to say that those who oppose the ordination of women believe that God is male – it is evident that God created a world of which sexuality is an integral part, and secondly that in the revelation of himself in and through human history he made use of the distinction between the sexes in the human race. I believe – and I speak now as one who believes there are theological objections – that he did so particularly to enable us to discern his relationship to us and our relationship to him. Thus, I do not and cannot believe that it was a mere accident of history that God was incarnate as a male, nor that the highest vocation of any created being was given to a female, Mary. I believe it is of abiding significance for a true understanding of the Gospel.

Thirdly, although in Christ male and female have equal access to God, the created distinctions between men and women were not abolished and we cannot try to behave as if they were. Although our

Lord tells us that in heaven there is neither marrying nor giving in marriage, he did not tell us to try and anticipate that situation but reaffirmed the teaching in Genesis which assumes the complementary and distinctive nature of the sexes in marriage. Equality does not mean identity and interchangeability. In the diversity of gifts in the church I would expect to find the distinction between the sexes which God used as the stuff of revelation reflected in the ordering of that part of the Body which is here on earth in space and time. Of that distinction and its relations to the priesthood, I shall have more to say later.

Meanwhile, what do I find when I look at the proponents' use of scripture? I have not time to quote the evidence for each of the statements I make, but I assure you that I can do so. First, I find the whole symbolism of both Old and New Testaments regarded simply as human inventions conditioned by the social and cultural conditions of the time. I say 'whole symbolism' because this notion is explicitly extended to include such fundamental symbolism as the Fatherhood of God and the Sonship of Christ. I find no suggestion that some symbols might be given by God as part of revelation to represent eternal truths and are therefore not negotiable. Secondly, I find an attitude which regards not only St Paul but our Lord himself as so conditioned by the cultural and social conditions of the time that he was incapable of transcending them. If both our Lord and St Paul were so conditioned, what about us? By what criteria do we judge that our conditioning in this century accords with the divine will but that in the earlier generations does not?

Thirdly, I find that there is no consistency among themselves in determining those parts of scripture of which we take account, and those which we discard as being culturally conditioned. The Bishop of Birmingham, for example, regards certain passages as self-evidently socially conditioned; whereas in the same volume Prof. Christopher Evans criticizes those who use self-evidence as ground for argument and points out that it is not convincing to those who do not agree. Such treatment of scripture seems to me to be quite alien to our Anglican tradition. As far as our Lord is concerned, it raises again the question 'Whom do men say that I am?' My answer must be 'Thou art the Christ, the Son of the living God who can say with authority "You have heard of old time but I say unto you".' Our Lord, to use a modern phrase, gave a new look to all he touched. The Lord of the gospels whom I know, love and seek to obey is not one who was socially conditioned in what he said or did.

When Bishop Ramsey asks, 'Does it serve the organic unity of the church in all its parts?', my answer must be a clear 'No' and for three reasons. First, it is clearly divisive, both in an ecumenical and in a domestic setting. Both the Roman Catholic Church, with whom the Archbishop of Canterbury has recently renewed his plea for intercommunion, and the Orthodox and Old Catholic Churches, have made their position clear. I am well aware of the speculations of some Roman Catholic theologians but I do not think it is honest or ecumenically charitable to latch on to them with the intention of discounting the proper authorities in their own church. May I remind the Synod that no one man has put the position of Rome more clearly or more charitably than Cardinal Hume when he addressed us earlier this year.

In the Anglican Communion there is division and distress which goes much deeper and is more widespread than is often made evident. We must not take advantage of the unwillingness of good men to go into schism and of their attempts to abide in charity with those whom they believe to be in error, and suppose that because they so act out of charity they do not care deeply and are not distressed. In ECUSA, for example, apart from the breakaway bodies which are considerably larger than is often stated, what is perhaps more significant is the fact, as I know from first-hand experience, that there is serious division within many dioceses and parishes. Others in the debate will, I hope, speak of the situation in Sweden, which presents us with a grave warning, and I do not think the facts will be quite as they were set out by the Bishop of Birmingham.

Secondly, I believe that, as has been so eloquently stated by the present Pope, the most urgent need of the church is renewed obedience to Christ as Lord. I now speak as one who believes that there are theological objections, and I must all too briefly indicate the basis for them. The 1662 Ordinal makes it clear beyond all question that the primary role of the priest is to represent the authority and headship of Christ as supreme for the church and for mankind. A priest stands for that divine headship, not for human headship which can properly be exercised by queens, abbesses, prime ministers. A priest stands for the fundamental headship of Christ from which all human headship, male and female, is derived and in obedience to which human headship must be exercised. To quote the World Council of Churches Faith and Order Paper *One*

Baptism, One Eucharist and A Mutually Recognized Ministry, 'The presence of this ministry in the community signifies the priority of divine initiative and authority in the Church's existence.' (I might mention in passing that I find no reference in the Ordinal to the priest being a representative of the people.)

I believe that the scriptures speak of God as Father, that Christ was incarnate as a male, that he chose men to be his apostles, in spite of breaking with tradition in his dealings with women, not because of social conditioning, but because in the order of creation headship and authority is symbolically and fundamentally associated with maleness. For the same reason, I believe that the highest vocation of any created being was given to a woman, Mary, as representative of mankind in our response to God because symbolically and fundamentally the response of sacrificial giving is associated with femaleness. I do not believe it is merely the result of social conditioning that in the scriptures, in the Jewish and Christian tradition, mankind and the church is presented as feminine to God, to whom our response must be one of obedience in contrast to those religions in which the divine is regarded as contained within creation and is to be manipulated or cajoled in order to provide what man needs. In other words, for a woman to represent the headship of Christ and the divine initiative would, unless her feminine gifts were obscured or minimized, evoke a different approach to God from those who worship. Instead of being reminded that we must respond in obedience to the divine initiative, a truth which I have learned in my evangelical upbringing which I have never forgotten, we should be tempted to suppose that we can take the initiative in our dealings with him.

For such a break with tradition we should expect overwhelmingly compelling reasons. Indeed I think that the question was wrongly put in the first place. We should not have been asked whether there were no fundamental objections. Rather we should have been asked to search scripture and tradition for compelling reasons for reversing the universal practice of the church for nearly two thousand years. Such reasons have not been forthcoming. On the contrary, I find that the arguments used lead me to question the rightness of an action which needs such arguments to justify it.

We are entitled to ask the advocates to convince us by sober and weighty argument, consonant with Anglican tradition, that beyond all reasonable doubt it would be theologically and morally right as Anglicans to proceed further.

For I speak as a convinced Anglican accepting that the Church of England is both catholic and reformed. When I admire Rome it is when she is faithful to scripture and the tradition of the undivided church. When I admire the reformed churches it is when they are faithful to scripture and the same tradition. I do not appeal to Rome or Constantinople nor Geneva as such; I appeal, as Anglicans have always appealed, to scripture and tradition and reason, tested by scripture.

I appreciate that the convictions on both sides are held deeply. Let me therefore end by quoting a great and wise Anglican, Archbishop Cyril Garbett. 'How', he asks, 'is legitimate to be distinguished from illegitimate development?' 'Not', he says, 'by an appeal to an infallible authority, to a General Council at some further unknown date or an appeal to antiquity which ignores changes in knowledge. The Church of England's answer' he says 'is that no new doctrine, opinion or practice may be accepted as necessary to salvation if it is opposed to the teaching of scripture. But any new interpretation or theory must be freely examined by the light of the scripture, tradition and the best knowledge of the day . . . The doctrinal position of the Church of England calls for intelligence, patience and humility. Intelligence so that God may be loved with the mind as well as the heart; patience to search and wait until the difficulties are removed and the truth is made clear; humility to listen to and reverence the roles of scripture and tradition.'

These are wise words. We shall not heed them if today we ignore our differences and commit the Church of England to action which we know must be divisive and also decisive. And whatever may be said, it is to action that we are asked to commit the Church of England. We may only be removing a barrier but that would indicate the way we are set to go. Too often in this Synod we have been told that to support a particular course of action will not commit us but merely leave the way open for a later decision, and then when the time comes for that decision we are told that it is not an open question because of the earlier vote. I ask that we now debate this in the deepest charity, forbearance and concern for truth, but I also submit that the only verdict in the present circumstances for the Church of England can be 'not proven', and that is no mandate to proceed. For these reasons I oppose the motion and for the sake of the Church of England and the church at large I ask the Synod to reject it.

Notes

Chapter 1   The Miracle of Convergence

1. Bernard and Margaret Pawley, *Rome and Canterbury through Four Centuries*, Mowbrays 1974.

2. Cf. B. and M. Pawley, op. cit. pp. 51–6.

3. Ibid., pp. 222–230, 261–277.

4. W. M. Abbott and J. Gallagher (eds), *The Documents of Vatican II, Decree on Ecumenism*, 6, Chapman 1966.

5. Ibid., 7.

6. Ibid., 24.

7. Cf. D. L. Edwards, *The British Churches Turn to the Future*, SCM Press 1973, p. 27.

8. *Sermons from Great St Mary's*, ed Hugh Montefiore, Collins 1968, p. 198.

9. G. D. Salmon, *The Infallibility of the Church*, revised and abridged by H. F. Woodhouse, John Murray 1952.

10. R. Hanson and R. Fuller, *The Church of Rome: A Dissuasive*, SCM Press 1948, p. 9.

11. Cited by B. and M. Pawley, op. cit., p. 231.

12. *The Easter People*, St Paul Publications 1980.

13. Cf. *Anglican-Roman Catholic Dialogues*, ed A. C. Clark and C. Davey, OUP 1974, p. 110.

14. Cf. *The Charismatic Movement in the Church of England*, CIO 1981, p. 7.

15. John XXIII, *Journal of a Soul*, Chapman 1964.

16. For an account of this pilgrimage, cf. W. Purcell, *Fisher of Lambeth*, Hodder and Stoughton 1969, pp. 268–288.

17. Ibid., p. 274.

18. Ibid., p. 283.

19. D. L. Edwards, op. cit., p. 17.

20. I am grateful to Professor C. N. L. Brooke, Dixie Professor of Ecclesiastical History in the University of Cambridge, for this information.

21. Cf. *Anglican-Roman Catholic Marriage*, CIO 1975, Section D, pp. 24ff. This was the Report of the Anglican-Roman Catholic International Commission on the Theology of Marriage and its Application to Mixed Marriages, a Commission set up after the Malta Report. Cf. also J. Trillo, *Marriage Between Anglicans and Roman Catholics*, CIO 1978, a report produced specifically for members of the Church of England.

22. Common Declaration of Pope Paul VI and Archbishop Michael Ramsey, printed in *Anglican-Roman Catholic Dialogues* ed A. C. Clark and C. Davey, OUP 1974, p. 2.

23. *Anglican Orthodox Dialogue (The Moscow Agreed Statement)*, SPCK 1977; *Anglican-Lutheran Dialogue (The Report of the European Commission)*, SPCK 1983; *God's Reign and our Unity (The Report of the Anglican-Reformed International Commission)*, SPCK 1984.

24. The point was made by Cardinal Ratzinger, Prefect of the Congregation of the Doctrine of the Faith, in a letter to Mgr Alan Clark, the Roman Catholic co-

chairman of ARCIC at the time when the Final Report was made public.

Chapter 2   The Church and its Sources of Authority

1. *Report of Proceedings*, General Synod, vol. 16, no. 1, p. 50.
2. Ibid., p. 52.
3. *Theology*, May 1977, p. 164.
4. *Theology*, September 1977, p. 327.
5. Ibid.
6. *Report of Proceedings*, General Synod, vol. 8, no. 1, p. 346.
7. The Doctrine Commission of the Church of England, *Christian Believing*, SPCK 1976.
8. *Report of Proceedings*, General Synod, vol. 8, no. 1, p. 354.
9. Anglican-Roman Catholic International Commission (ARCIC), *The Final Report*, Authority in the Church I, para. 2, SPCK/CTS 1982, p. 52.
10. Ibid., Elucidation, para. 2, p. 69.
11. Ibid., Elucidation, para. 3, pp. 71f.
12. J. Ratzinger, 'Anglican-Catholic Dialogue', *Insight*, vol. 1, no. 3, March 1983, p. 6.
13. *The Final Report*, Elucidation, para. 3, p. 70.
14. Ibid., Authority in the Church I, para. 14, p. 59.
15. Ibid., Authority in the Church II, para. 27, p. 93.
16. Ibid., Elucidation, para. 2, p. 70.
17. Ratzinger, art. cit., p. 4.
18. *The Final Report*, Elucidation, para. 3, p. 72.
19. W. M. Abbott & J. Gallagher (eds), *The Documents of Vatican II*, Introduction to the *Constitution on Divine Revelation* by R. A. F. Mackenzie SJ, Chapman 1966, p. 108.
20. Ibid., *Constitution on Divine Revelation*, 9.
21. Ibid., *Constitution on Divine Revelation*, 10.
22. E. Amand de Mendieta, *Rome and Canterbury*, Jenkins 1962, pp. 143f.
23. Cf. the Lambeth Conferences of 1948 and 1968 for the same sources of authority, as noted in ARCIC, *The Final Report*, Authority in the Church I, p. 61 (footnote).
24. 'According to the ancient law and usage of this Church and Realm of England, the inferior clergy who have received authority to minister in any diocese owe canonical obedience in all things lawful and right to the bishop of the same . . . (Canon C 1 3.)
25. F. Paget, *Introduction to the Fifth Book of Hooker's Ecclesiastical Polity*, OUP 1899, p. 114.
26. *Doctrine in the Church of England*, SPCK 1938, p. 6. Reissued 1982, with a new preface by Geoffrey Lampe.
27. Ibid., p. 39.
28. David Holloway, *The Church of England – Where is it Going?*, Kingsway Publications 1985, p. 112.
29. Cf. *Subscription and Assent to the 39 Articles*, SPCK 1968.
30. Stephen Sykes, *The Integrity of Anglicanism*, Mowbray 1978, pp. 37f.
31. *Christian Believing*, SPCK 1976.
32. Ibid., pp. 35–38.
33. *Believing in the Church*, SPCK 1981.
34. *Christian Believing*, p. 47.
35. Ibid., p. 48.
36. Ibid., p. 50.
37. Sykes, op. cit., p. 33.

38. Ibid., p. 13.

39. Letter to *The Times*, 1 June 1977, quoted by Sykes, op. cit., pp. 110f.

40. *The Lambeth Conference 1948*, SPCK 1948, Part II, p. 84.

41. *Doctrine in the Church of England*, p. 38.

42. *The Lambeth Conference 1948*, pp. 84ff.

43. Quoted by G. Leonard, 'Christian Decision Making', *The Synod of Westminster* ed P. Moore, SPCK 1986, p. 106.

44. Ratzinger, art. cit., p. 2.

45. Clifford Longley in *The Times*, 12 December 1985.

46. ARCIC, *The Final Report*, Authority in the Church II, para. 12, p. 86.

47. Ratzinger, art. cit., p. 5.

48. Sacred Congregation for the Doctrine of the Faith, *Observations on the Final Report of the Anglican-Roman Catholic International Commission*, CTS 1982, p. 12.

49. *Documents of Vatican II, Constitution on the Church*, 8.

50. *Documents of Vatican II, Decree on Ecumenism*, 13.

51. ARCIC, *The Final Report*, Authority in the Church II, para. 22, note 2.

Chapter 3 The Church and its Structures of Authority

1. ARCIC, *The Final Report*, Eucharistic Doctrine: Elucidation, para. 9, p. 24.

2. Ibid., Ministry and Ordination: Elucidation, para. 6, pp. 44f.

3. J. J. Hughes, *Absolutely Null and Utterly Void*, Sheed and Ward 1968.

4. Cf. F. E. Brightman, *What Objections have been made to Anglican Orders?*, SPCK 1896.

5. Cf. *Anglican Orders: The Bull of His Holiness Leo XIII and the Answer of the Archbishops of England*, SPCK 1943.

6. F. Clark, *Anglican Orders and Defect of Intention*, London 1956; *Eucharistic Sacrifice and the Reformation*, London 1960.

7. Cf. J. J. Hughes, op. cit., pp. 288f.

8. Ibid., p. 292.

9. *The Final Report*, Ministry and Ordination: Elucidation, para. 6, p. 45.

10. Ibid., Authority in the Church I, para. 5, p. 54.

11. Ibid., para. 7, p. 55.

12. *The Documents of Vatican II, Dogmatic Constitution on the Church*, 20.

13. Ibid., 21.

14. Ibid., 28.

15. Ibid., 23.

16. Ibid., 27.

17. *The Documents of Vatican II, Decree on the Bishop's Pastoral Office in the Church*, 36.

18. J. Ratzinger, 'Anglican-Catholic Dialogue', *Insight*, vol. 1, no. 3, March 1983, p. 2.

19. Ibid., p. 7.

20. Ibid.

21. P. G. H. Thomas, 'Some Principles of Anglican Authority', *Authority in the Anglican Communion*, Anglican Consultative Council 1981, pp. 23f.

22. *The Final Report*, Authority in the Church I, para. 13, p. 58.

23. Cf. T. Bradshaw, 'Primacy and Authority in the ARCIC Report', *Theology*, January 1986, pp. 26ff.

24. *The Final Report*, Authority in the Church I, para. 16, p. 60.

25. Ibid., para. 19, p. 62.

26. Ibid., Elucidation, para. 3, p. 71.

27. *Towards a Church of England Response to BEM and ARCIC*, CIO 1985, paras. 238, 240, p. 92.

28. Ibid.
29. *The Final Report*, Authority in the Church II, para, 28. p. 94.
30. Ratzinger, art. cit., p. 5.
31. Bishops' Conference of England and Wales, *Response to the Final Report of the Anglican-Roman Catholic International Commission*, CTS 1985, para. 40.
32. *The Final Report*, Authority in the Church II, paras. 19, 20, p. 90.
33. *Dogmatic Constitution on the Church*, 22.
34. Ibid.
35. *The Final Report*, Authority in the Church II, para. 6, p. 83.
36. Bishops' Conference of England and Wales, op. cit., para. 39.
37. *The Final Report*, Authority in the Church II, para. 12, p. 86.
38. *Dogmatic Constitution on the Church*, 25.
39. *Towards a Church of England Response to BEM and ARCIC*, para. 232, p. 89.
40. Ibid., para. 249, p. 95.
41. *Christian Believing*, SPCK 1976, pp. 43–51.
42. *The Final Report*, Authority in the Church II, para. 12, p. 86.
43. Ratzinger, art. cit., p. 5.
44. Co-chairmen's Preface to Authority in the Church I, p. 50.

Chapter 4   The Church and the Laity

1. K. Bliss, *We the People*, SCM Press 1963.
2. H. Chadwick, 'A Brief Apology for Authority in the Church' *Theology*, September 1977, p. 330.
3. ARCIC, *The Final Report*, Authority in the Church I, para. 6, p. 54.
4. Ibid.
5. *The Final Report*, Elucidation, para. 3, p. 72.
6. *The Final Report*, Authority in the Church II, para. 31, p. 97.
7. *Documents of Vatican II, Dogmatic Constitution on the Church*, 3.
8. Ibid., 33.
9. Ibid., 31.
10. Ibid., 32.
11. *Documents of Vatican II, Decree on the Apostolate of the Laity*, 24.
12. *Pro Vita Mundi: Dossiers*, Dossier 6, Brussels 1979, p. 2.
13. *Decree on the Apostolate of the Laity*, 29.
14. Ibid., 31.
15. S. Sykes, *Authority in the Anglican Communion*, Anglican Consultative Council 1981, p. 11.
16. *In the House of the Living God*, Catholic Information Services, Abbots Langley 1982, p. 9.
17. The status of episcopal conferences was a subject of major importance at the Extraordinary Synod held in Rome in November 1985. The final report of the Synod, while describing them as an expression of *affectus collegialis*, recommended them for further study. Cf. P. Hebblethwaite, *Synod Extraordinary*, Darton Longman and Todd 1986, p. 137.
18. C. Davis, *The Downside Review*, October 1963, pp. 307–16.
19. A. Dyson, 'Clericalism, Church and Laity', *All are Called*, CIO 1985, p. 15.
20. J. A. T. Robinson, *The New Reformation?*, SCM Press 1965, p. 67.
21. M. Gibbs, 'Laity Training', *Layman's Church*, Lutterworth Press 1963, p. 77.
22. *Report of Proceedings*, General Synod, vol. 16, February 1985, p. 249.
23. Ibid., p. 75.

Chapter 5   The Mother of God Incarnate

1. Cf. R. Laurentin, *Structure et Theologie Luc 1–11*, Paris 1957, pp. 64–90.

2. Cf. E. Hennecke, *New Testament Apocrypha* Vol I, SCM Press 1963, pp. 370ff.

3. Sermo 186, 1. For a discussion of Mary's virginity *in partu* and *post partum*, cf. G. Miegge, *The Virgin Mary*, Lutterworth Press 1955, pp. 36–52.

4. Cf. Jerome, *Adversus Helvidium*.

5. Miegge, op. cit., p. 77.

6. Cf. J. B. Jaggar, *The Immaculate Conception*, Catholic Truth Society 1944, p. 2. It is said that 50,000 copies of this pamphlet had been sold.

7. Cf. N. P. Williams, *The Ideas of the Fall and Original Sin*, London 1929.

8. Cf. Tischendorf cited by V. Bennett and R. Winch, *The Assumption of Our Lady and Catholic Theology*, SPCK 1950, p. 25.

9. *Concerning the Glory of Martyrdom, PL* 71, 708.

10. *Doctrine in the Church of England*, SPCK 1938, pp. 82f. The position has not been materially changed by the *Statement* of the House of Bishops published in June 1986 in response to a General Synod debate on the nature of belief, which had been provoked by statements made by Dr David Jenkins, when Bishop-designate of Durham, concerning the virginal conception of Jesus and his physical resurrection. The Bishops 'acknowledge and uphold' the virginal conception of Jesus 'as expressing the faith of the Church of England'. But at the same time they affirm that they are responsible for guarding, expounding and teaching the faith 'in ways which will effectively "proclaim it afresh in each generation"', while at the same time distinguishing in our teaching the ideas of theological exploration from the beliefs which are the corporate teaching of the church'. The Bishops further assert that the relation between tradition and enquiry 'has always meant that there can be a proper diversity in the understanding and expression of the Christian faith'.

11. Rosemary Radford Ruether, *Mary – The Feminine Face of the Church*, SCM Press 1979, pp. 28f.

12. ARCIC, *The Final Report*, Authority in the Church II, para. 30, pp. 95f.

Chapter 6   Traditions of Ethical Thinking

1. R. C. Mortimer, *Elements of Moral Theology*, A. & C. Black 1947.

2. D. Rhymes, *No New Morality*, Constable 1964.

3. *Humanae Vitae*, 1968, para. 4.

4. Cf. H. Montefiore, 'Is Interest Immoral?' *Banking World*, December 1984, pp. 18f.

5. All Reports of the Church of England Board for Social Responsibility are published by the Church Information Office, unless otherwise acknowledged.

6. *Pacem in Terris*, 1963, paras. 8–27.

7. *Human Rights: Our Understanding and Our Responsibilities*, General Synod 324, January 1977.

8. Ibid., para. 33.

9. *On Dying Well*, CIO 1975, pp. 61f.

10. *The Challenge of Peace*, CTS/SPCK 1983.

11. *Force in the Modern World*, General Synod 168; *Christians in a Violent World*, General Synod 414.

12. *The Church and the Bomb*, Hodder 1982.

13. *Report of Proceedings*, General Synod, vol. 14, no. 1, February 1983, p. 302.

14. *Faith in the City*, A Call for Action by Church and Nation, Church House Publishing 1985.

Chapter 7   The Church and Sexual Ethics

1. *Anglican-Roman Catholic Marriage*, CIO/Infoform 1975, para. 21.

2. Ibid.

3. Cf. *Marriage, Divorce and the Church*, SPCK 1971: *Marriage and the Church's Task*, CIO 1978.

4. In the diocese of Birmingham in 1985 2854 marriages were solemnized in parish churches, of which 251 were 'remarriages' while the former spouse of a partner was still living.

5. *Lambeth Conferences (1867–1939)*, SPCK 1948, p. 51.

6. Ibid., p.50.

7. Ibid., p. 166.

8. *The Lambeth Conference 1958*, SPCK 1959, part I, p. 57.

9. *Humanae Vitae*, para. 11.

10. Ibid., para. 15.

11. *Lambeth Conferences (1867–1930)*, p. 200.

12. *The Lambeth Conference 1958*, part 2, p. 14.

13. *Humanae Vitae*, para. 14.

14. Ibid., para. 3.

15. O. O'Donovan, *Begotten or Made?*, Clarendon Press 1984, p. 77.

16. Quoted by J. Mahoney, *Bioethics and Belief*, Sheed and Ward 1984, pp. 68ff., from which the following quotations are also taken.

17. Cf. *Abortion – An Ethical Discussion*, CIO 1965, p. 27.

18. Ibid., p. 30.

19. *Report of Proceedings*, Church Assembly, vol. XLVI, no. 1, Spring 1966, p. 116.

20. *Report of Proceedings*, General Synod, vol. 14, no. 2, July 1983, pp. 815f.

21. Comnd 9314, HMSO 1984.

22. *In Vitro Fertilization – Morality and Public Policy*, Evidence Submitted by the Catholic Bishops' Joint Committee on Bioethical Issues, nd, p. 15.

23. *Human Fertilization and Embryology. The Response of the Board for Social Responsibility of the Church of England*, CIO 1984.

24. *Personal Origins*, CIO 1985.

25. Mahoney, op. cit., p. 81.

26. *Sexual Ethics*, CTS 1975, para. 8.

27. *Homosexual Relations: A Contribution to Discussion*, CIO 1979. An excellent survey of the whole subject was later published in P. Coleman, *Christian Attitudes to Homosexuality*, SPCK 1980.

28. *Report of Proceedings*, General Synod, vol. 12, no. 1, February 1981, p. 415.

29. Ibid., p. 453.

30. *Sexual Ethics*, para. 9.

31. *Humanae Vitae*, para. 14.

32. *Sterilization: An Ethical Enquiry*, CIO 1962, p. 25.

33. *Report of Proceedings*, General Synod, vol. 10, no. 3, November 1979, p. 1052.

34. Ibid., p. 1045.

35. *Observations on the Final Report of the Anglican-Roman Catholic International Commission*, CTS 1982, C.(2).

Chapter 8   Women and the Ministerial Priesthood

1. *Gender and Ministry*, CIO 1962.

2. *Report of the Archbishop's Commission on Women and Holy Orders*, CIO 1966.

3. Resolution 34.

4. Much of this literature is listed in the notes to 'The Theology of Priesthood', *Yes to Women Priests*, ed. H Montefiore, Mowbray 1978, pp. 12ff.

5. *Women and the Priesthood*, CTS 1977.

6. 'Women and the Priesthood', *The Month*, March 1977, p. 76.
7. *Women and the Priesthood*, part 4.
8. *The Month*, art. cit.
9. St Thomas, *In IV Sent.*, dist. 25, g. 2, quaestionuncula 1 ad 4.
10. *The Month*, art. cit.
11. *Women and the Priesthood*, part 5.
12. *Sacerdotium Ministeriale*, CTS 1983, para. 4.
13. *The Month*, art. cit.
14. For a more recent example of Roman Catholic dissent, see the support by the two distinguished Jesuits, Dr R. Butterworth SJ and Dr Robert Murray SJ to the Open Letter to the Bishop of London from Richard Harries, Dean of King's College, London (January 1986). The letter was subsequently published in *The Tablet*, 8 February 1986.
15. John Austin Baker, 'Eucharistic Presidency and Women's Ordination', *Theology*, September 1985, pp. 350ff.
16. Ibid., p. 354.
17. *Decree Concerning the Most Holy Eucharist*, c. 2.
18. *Constitution on the Sacred Liturgy*, c. 7
19. *Mysterium Fidei*, CTS 1965, para. 49.
20. *Summa Theologica* III q. 83, a. 1, ad 3.
21. *In IV Sent.*, dist. 25, q. 2, a. 2, q^{a}1, ad 4.
22. Official Commentary, *Briefing*, 5 February 1977, p. 13
23. ARCIC, *The Final Report*, p. 44.
24. Report, para. 7, privately published. The Consultation took place at Versailles, 27 February–3 March 1978.
25. *Women and the Priesthood*, part 4.

Chapter 9   The Limits of Pluralism

1. Donald Schon, *Beyond the Stable State*, Temple Smith 1971, p. 108.
2. Ibid., pp. 111f.
3. E. Best, *One Body in Christ*, SPCK 1955, p. 136. Contrast J. A. T. Robinson, *The Body*, SCM Press 1952, pp. 50f.
4. Ibid., p. 98.
5. *Dogmatic Constitution on the Church*, 23.
6. Ibid.
7. The sermon was published in *The Tablet*, 24 January 1970, pp. 72f.
8. *Decree on Ecumenism*, 14.
9. H. Küng, *The Church*, Burns and Oates 1967, p. 343.
10. Cf. P. Avis, *Ecumenical Theology*, SPCK 1986, pp. 8f.
11. H. Küng, *The Structures of the Church*, Burns and Oates 1964, p. 349.
12. *Dogmatic Constitution on the Church*, 22.
13. It is perhaps appropriate for this suggestion to emanate from an Anglican, for the Anglican Communion has obvious points of connection with the British Commonwealth of Nations, just as the Roman Catholic Church is not without similarities to the old Roman imperial system.